In the Shadow of Lightcliffe's Old Tower

Two Churches and a Churchyard.

Dorothy Barker and Ian Philp

Lightcliffe and District Local History Society

Published 2022 by Lightcliffe & District Local History Society
https://www.lightcliffehistory.org.uk
Copyright Dorothy Barker and Ian Philp © 2021

The rights of Dorothy Barker and Ian Philp to be identified
as the authors of this work
have been asserted by them in accordance with
the Copyright, Designs and Patents Act of 1988

ISBN 978-1-9162983-2-3

Printed by Amadeus Press, Ezra House, West 26 Business Park,
Cleckheaton, West Yorkshire, BD19 4TQ.
www.amadeuspress.co.uk

In the Shadow of Lightcliffe's Old Tower

Two Churches and a Churchyard.

Contents

Foreword

I find it impossible to think of St Matthew's churchyard without bringing to mind Gray's *Elegy Written in a Country Churchyard*, where

Each in his narrow cell forever laid,
The rude Forefathers of the hamlet sleep.

At least 11,000 of our forebears have been buried in this acre and a half since 1674, the year of the first recorded interment. However, the first Eastfield Chapel was built in 1529, so we can assume that many more villagers, old and young, of Lightcliffe and beyond, lie here in their narrow cells.

By no means all the incumbents are anonymous, with their 'homely joys and destiny obscure'. One of the benefactors of the original chapel was the Rookes family, perpetuated in the halls, lane and wood of Norwood Green which bear their name.

The Walker family, who owned most of Lightcliffe until Evan Charles Sutherland Walker, then of Crow Nest, sold much of it off in 1867, provided the major part of the cost of the first St Matthew's Church in 1775. As we know well, only the tower remains. The family's best-known member is Ann, partner of Anne Lister of Shibden Hall. She is buried here alongside her ancestors.

A century after the original St Matthew's, the 'new' church was erected up the road, again largely through the generosity of a local resident, Major Johnston Jonas Foster of Cliffe Hill, son of the founder of Black Dyke Mills, Queensbury.

All this, and much, much more has emerged through the extensive and meticulous research of Dorothy Barker and Ian Philp. We are reminded of Joseph Naylor, who took his horse to the Crimea and back, Colonel Joshua Guest who defended Edinburgh Castle from the Jacobites in 1745, the Holmes family of Smith House and the Watkinsons of Woodfield House. There are those who lived long lives, and, tragically, so many whose years were cut short by diseases now eradicated, by accidents at work, particularly in quarrying, and the terrible litany of young men who perished in the First World War.

Read this outstanding work of scholarship with relish, acquaint yourself with distinguished villagers of long ago, but above all, wander around the churchyard with humility as you consider those whose names are lost forever, and reflect on 'the short and simple annals of the poor'.

Bob Horne
Chair, Lightcliffe & District Local History Society
November 2021

Introduction

In 2012 much of the churchyard was totally overgrown with brambles, rosebay willowherb and saplings. The paths were ill-defined and for much of the year difficult to walk along. The headstones were covered by the undergrowth and anyone searching for a grave would have struggled. The grass area surrounding the tower was cut by the Council and even the new part where burials currently take place was largely desolate.

A neighbour, Angela Monaghan, together with the vicar, Rev Kathryn Buck, held a public meeting and from that the Friends of St Matthew's Churchyard group was formed.

This group of volunteers began the daunting task of clearing the undergrowth and revealing paths and headstones. Over the next few years, with grants from the Council, the Heritage Lottery Fund, donations and money raised from annual concerts, the Friends were able to buy equipment, establish a website, restore some of the headstones and build a database of all of the 11,000 burials that have taken place since the late 1600s.

Old graves near the tower, many of which were covered by grass, have been cleared as have all of the headstones throughout the rest of the churchyard and all have been photographed. The burial records have been transcribed and recorded in a searchable way on the website so that family members who are looking for graves can now find them.

As these records became easily available so did the stories behind many of those buried here.

This book traces the history of the two churches in Lightcliffe and tries to bring to life many individuals and families associated with St Matthew's. For both church and people buried in the churchyard, we have concentrated on the period from 1785 to around 1930 with a few exceptions.

Towards the end of the book, we provide a guide to the churchyard for visitors.

Dorothy Barker and Ian Philp 2021

Notes on Place Names.

The names of places sometimes change over time and Cliff Hill is a prime example. In 1798 we have Cliffhill, Anne Lister calls it cliff-hill, the burial records for both Ann Walkers (1847 and 1854) show Cliff Hill but a few years later it is referred to as Cliffe Hill. Other examples include Bailiff (e) Bridge and Li(y)dgate. We use the version that best matches the place at the time in question.

1 History of the Churches and Churchyard

The old church.

Our two churches and the churchyard lie in the village of Lightcliffe about three miles east of Halifax. Until 1869 it was part of the very large parish of Halifax.

The original Eastfield Chapel was built on land given by Richard Rookes in 1529. The land lay at the junction of the Wakefield to Halifax highway and a cartway leading from Brighouse to the mill in Coley. It was funded by William Rookes and several other landowners in the area. There are no contemporary drawings of this chapel but it would have been a simple structure, possibly with a bell at the western end.

Lightcliffe, at the time, was a very small community of a few houses, farmhouses, cottages, and acres of open land and woods. There would have been a very clear distinction between it and Hipperholme. It was in the very large parish of Halifax so the nearest place of worship would have been the Parish Church (now a Minster) in Halifax some 3 to 4 miles away. The chapel would have made it easier for the inhabitants to worship locally, although everyone was expected to attend for at least one communion each year in Halifax. Initially, it was Roman Catholic for a few years of its existence but then became an Anglican church. Its story is told by J. Horsfall Turner.

Our story begins as this chapel was replaced by a more substantial building in the 1770s. There had been an assessment of the fabric of the chapel with a view to improve it but the decision made was to rebuild, and permission (a Faculty) was granted by the Bishop's Court in 1774. The population of the village had doubled between 1720 and 1770 and continued to grow rapidly. This would have been another reason for a new church. The Faculty was granted to Rev Richard Sutcliffe, curate, and to William Walker and William Sutcliffe as churchwardens.

The architect is unknown, but Nicholas Pevsner in his West Riding edition of 'Buildings of England' says that it is built in the style of John Carr of York. We do know that it was built by William Mallinson, who is buried within a few yards of the tower.

Sacred to the memory of William Mallinson, late of Halifax, Mason,
who erected this chapel in the year of our Lord 1775 and died in 1798 aged 48 years.
Stand Reader Here and Spend a Tear
and think of me who now lies here ...

It was largely funded by William Walker of Crow Nest mansion, including the importation of timber from the Baltic for the roofs of the church, Crow Nest and Cliffe Hill mansions. It is said he went to the Baltic himself to supervise the purchase and also that the timbers were amongst the first large loads transported from the Humber to Brighouse using the Aire Calder Navigation canal system.

An advert was placed in *The Leeds Intelligencer* on 22nd April 1774 looking for tradesman. Under the heading of Lightcliffe Chapel in the Parish of Halifax it read:

> *Notice is hereby given, That any Mason, Carpenter, Joiner, Glazier or Plasterer willing to undertake his respective Branch of Work in rebuilding the said Chapel may apply to William Walker, Esq of Crow Nest near Lightcliffe on Friday next betwixt the hours of One and Four in the Afternoon.*

St Matthew's was a mid-Georgian preaching box with an octagonal open stone cupola on the otherwise plain tower. Square cut ashlar stone was used for much of the building. Almost certainly local sandstone would have been used because of its quality and the avoidance of transport cost. One reference states that the stone came from quarries at Hove Edge. The building was approximately 57 feet long and 36 feet wide. The radius of the apse was 12 feet; the tower about 60 feet high with sides of around 13 feet. A small vestry, with a sloping roof, was attached to the northern side of the tower with direct access to the church. The bell in the tower was dated 1604 so would have transferred from the original chapel to this church.

After entering the church through the eastern door (both doors were on the south side) and having noted the date carved above the doors – 1775 (actually carved about 50 years later by a John Sykes and costing 2 shillings) – a visitor would see a simple church. There was minimum decoration and just a few memorial tablets.

The quatrefoil columns supporting the gallery were in cast iron. This makes them exceptionally early. Although Sir Christopher Wren was responsible for the use of cast iron columns as early as the 1690s in the House of Commons, the earliest surviving example of this material as gallery supports is at the church of St James, Toxteth, in Liverpool. And the dates are virtually identical: St James's was begun in 1774 and finished 1775; Lightcliffe seems to have been an exact contemporary. Ironbridge in Shropshire was also built at this time.

This plain interior was altered in the 1860s as a result of gifts from Evan Charles Sutherland Walker (William Walker's great grandson). From then there would have been few, if any, changes until the church was demolished. This is rare, because soon after these alterations, the planning began for the new church and further changes would not have been considered. Once the new church was consecrated, the old church was used infrequently,

and only basic maintenance would have taken place. The photographs taken just before demolition and descriptions in Horsfall Turner's history show how the church would have looked from the 1860s.

The pulpits were presented by Sutherland Walker, as was the plain deal communion table, on which would have stood chalice, flagon and paten plate. One chalice dates from 1570 and was made in Dorset, another was given by Martha Sutcliffe, the widow of the curate when this church was built, and a flagon and paten are dated 1823/24. The churchwardens' staves, now in the parish church, may be from here.

To the north there was a reading pulpit which covered the vault where Ann Walker and others were previously buried, and to the south was the preaching pulpit. The eastern most ground-floor window was blocked up and used for the plaque dedicated to Ann Walker and members of Evan Charles Sutherland Walker's family. The east end was a shallow apse with a Venetian window with delicate rococo plasterwork.

On the north side of the east window was written the Lord's Prayer and the Commandments I-IV. To the south was The Apostles' Creed and the Commandments V-X.

The east window was presented by Sutherland Walker in memory of his parents George Mackay Sutherland and Elizabeth (Walker), a young son, and Ann Walker. It was made in Edinburgh. The central theme is the Lord's Supper, the left-hand one is Christ welcoming children and the right, the Good Samaritan. The image is an impression by artist Hilary Griffiths.

At ground level there was a series of box pews. On three sides, supported by cast iron columns and framework, was a gallery of further pews. The interior of Heywood Chapel, Northowram, is similarly constructed (1836) as is that at St Matthew's Rastrick (1798) especially in terms of boxed pews in the gallery and the plain apse.

The walls were plainly decorated. There was little heating, though E.C. Sutherland Walker provided a small stove heater near the pulpits. Even in the 1870s there was little lighting. Horsfall-Turner states that the font was given in 1866 by Daniel Carter of Giles House. However, there is a receipt for E.C. Sutherland Walker for £25 for a Caen font and its pedestal. The earlier one, apparently, became a flower stand at Crow Nest.

The organ was a Schnetzler organ. Schnetzler was a Swiss-born, London-based organ builder who had built organs in Cambridge, Yale, Hull, Ludlow, Beverley and Halifax Parish Church before tackling Lightcliffe! The one in Halifax Parish Church would have been played by William Herschel, the astronomer who discovered Uranus, when he was organist there in 1760. He is reputed to have given music lessons to William Walker junior and his sister Elizabeth Walker, later Priestley. Perhaps having played on or at least heard the Halifax organ, the Walker family was keen to have a Schnetzler organ in Lightcliffe's newly built church.

The organ was described as having a mahogany case with gilt pipes in front and with glass doors, 5 draw knobs each side from GG to F (omitting GG sharp), a manual, 7 stops and 350 pipes.

The first official performance was of *The Messiah* on 24th August 1787 with organist, Mr Stopford. Another church organist for many years was Mr George Lister who was also a bassoon player and composer of some note. Both William Walker junior and his nephew William Priestley were keen musicians who also gave recitals in the newly built church. The organ was still playable in 1960 though out of tune.

In September 1833 a concert was given to benefit the widow and family of Robert Sladdin, cordwainer and singer, at which Susan Sykes made her singing debut. She became Mrs Sunderland, known now for the annual Huddersfield festival bearing her name. She sang twice before Queen Victoria and was known as Yorkshire's Queen of Song. Her father and brother were local gardeners.

The pews were largely owned by families, but there were some for the poor. Some near the front were lined and upholstered in red material. They were numbered and named and the small plaques are stored, with other material, in Wakefield West Yorkshire Archives. Photographs are on the churchyard website.

The first Appendix summarises who owned which pew and where they were when the church was rebuilt.

There is a story that the local constables had pews near the back, by the door. Their job included rounding up those who were missing the service. They left their pew just as the sermon was beginning and returned as it concluded. Remember there was an expectation at that time that everyone attended church.

The tower has a stone staircase up two flights and then wooden steps. The first flight gave access to the gallery, the second, narrower flight led to the winding mechanism for the clock. It had a single bell with a single clock face pointing south. The bell of 15" diameter was cast by William Oldfield of Doncaster & York in 1604. It disappeared well before the church itself was demolished. Inside the tower and above the first ceiling is the inscribed stone from the original chapel, the dedication reads

Deo et Sancto Mattaeo.
Apostolo Evangelistae
Martyri Sacra
A.D. DCXXIX
'to God & St Matthew, apostle, evangelist, sacred martyr 1529'

Now stored (vertically) within the tower is the Benefactors' Board. Originally it was on the western wall. It gave details of those local landowners who provided charitable funds for the poor of the parish.

- Thomas Whiteley, 1631, of Cinder Hills – Yew Tree Farm and Harley Head Farm
- Nathaniel Waterhouse, 1642, (of Waterhouse Almshouses)
- Sam Sunderland 1671, of Harden Beck Bingley and Coley Hall – Birks Close Farm, Norwood Green
- Michael Gibson, 1738, Slead Hall, on Pear Tree Farm
- Richard Sutcliffe, 1782, on Sheard Green, Hove Edge
- Jas Gledhill, 1789, Smith House
- William Walker, 1810, Cliff Hill and Crow Nest

That for Richard Sutcliffe shows that the farm and land that he owned in Hove Edge was to provide 20 shillings each year for distribution to 20 poor people of the parish at Christmas.

Within the tower, for safe keeping, are memorials to members of the Walker family including John (a beautifully sculpted Greek profile) and Ann, and to Rev Richard Sutcliffe, curate when the church was built.

We know some things about the running of St Matthew's, as in the Archives in Wakefield there are churchwardens' accounts. A typical extract, written by Samuel Washington as a churchwarden, tells us the cost of communion wine (5s per bottle), the payment of £5 5s as the salary of Sydney Ellis as parish clerk, 14s for the washing of surplices, 7s 4d for the cost of winding the clock and £1 8s 6d for Samuel Sowden as sexton.

For much of its existence Lightcliffe was part of the Halifax Parish, said to be the largest in England. The curate was paid by the local congregation, additionally with monies provided by the Queen Anne's Bounty which had been set up to support local Anglican clergy. Our curate had the income from farms at Sheard Green in Hove Edge and two farms, one in Northowram and one near Heptonstall. In addition, quit rents (a form of land tax) were paid on local houses, German, Smith, Giles, Lower Cliffe Hill, Yew Trees and Lidgegate (Lidgate) and several farms in Norwood Green. The value of the living in 1860 was £150 and the local population was around 2,400.

In 1846 *The London Gazette* reported that Lightcliffe was to become a chapelry within the parish and its boundaries were defined. These included Mytholm, up to close to Coley, across Norwood Green and up towards North Bierley. From there down to the edge of the hamlet of Brighouse before crossing back round Hove Edge to Mytholm. During the time that it was a chapelry the curate received half of the fees for baptisms, marriages and burials with the other half going to the vicar of Halifax. St Matthew's became a parish in its own right in 1869 and in 1909, when the parish of Northowram was created, there was a small alteration to the boundary.

The fate of the old church

During the last few years of its life there are several comments in the parish magazine regarding the church's fate. Rev Frank White had been trying to find alternative uses for the church since the late 1950s. As services took place in the new church, old St Matthew's was only used as a mortuary chapel and for the occasional service; for instance, we know that in the late 1940s and early 1950s, a service was held at 3pm on Whit Sunday. The organ played, with volunteer youngsters pumping the bellows, and the choir sang. It was damaged by storms in the 1960s and vandals and thieves began to destroy the fabric. By the late 1960s there were serious concerns regarding the safety of the building. The Diocese wanted to demolish the entire church following a newly passed Pastoral Measure of 1969 under which decisions over the fate of disused Anglican churches were systematised for the first time. This was when an organisation called Friends of Friendless Churches stepped in. In April 1971, Rev White was able to report that the church would be demolished and that the contract specified that great care was to be observed so that the vaults beneath the nave would not be damaged. A recent archaeological survey over the site of the church indicated that this had been done.

The body of the church was demolished at the expense of the Diocese but the cost of repairing the tower and making good its newly exposed eastern elevation and that of the flank where the lean-to vestry used to sit was met by Friends of Friendless Churches. As this was the first ever vesting of the newly established Friendless Churches Trust, the financial challenge was acute. The tower was passed formally to the Friends on a 99-year lease on 1st January 1974. The reconstruction of the eastern façade and other repairs were carried out by Marshalls of Elland at a cost of £10,000. Further repairs, particularly to the cupola, were carried out in 1990 costing £5,800. It is a Grade II listed building. The photograph shows the demolition when the main body of the church had gone leaving the tower and part of the west wall

The new church

When Major Johnston Jonas Foster of the Black Dyke Mills family bought Cliffe Hill mansion at the 1867 Crow Nest auction, he also purchased Green House and the adjoining plot for £1270. The plots lay between Cliffe Hill and Wakefield Road and are 300m from the churchyard. The house and outbuildings were demolished, and the new St Matthew's church built, together with the terrace now called Greenhouses.

The main reasons for a new church would probably have been the difficulties of maintaining and modernising the old church, providing a church more in tune with the changes in liturgical practices, possibly even a desire to have a church as grand as the recently built Congregational Church on the Leeds and Whitehall Road, partly financed by Sir Titus Salt, Foster's neighbour at Crow Nest and fellow textile magnate.

Major Foster was willing to provide funds for every aspect of the church but was persuaded by the vicar and churchwardens that others would wish to contribute. He willingly acceded to this suggestion. His contribution was around £15,000 (£16 million today).

The architect was W. Swinden Barber (1832-1908), a Brighouse man, who specialised in Gothic Revival and Arts and Crafts. His work included several churches and some secular buildings in West Yorkshire. A characteristic of many of his designs was crenellations, as seen here. His clerk of works was William Ridgway, and the masons were Luke and William Crowther of Brighouse. The overall style is perpendicular gothic and built in local sandstone.

S. Matthews Church LIGHTCLIFFE. built by Major Foster W.S.Barber Architect

The laying of the foundation stone by Mrs Jonas Foster took place on September 16th 1873. During the ceremony there was a serious accident when the crane lifting the stone broke and part of it fell on several members of the crowd. Elizabeth Kershaw suffered a fractured spine, Mrs Pyrah had her thigh and shoulder fractured and others sustained less serious injuries.

The New Church, Lightcliffe, Hipperholme.

Two years later, on September 21st 1875, the church was consecrated by The Lord Bishop of Ripon. Forty to fifty churchmen, led by Bishop Ryan, the Archdeacon of Craven, processed from the National School (Lightcliffe Primary School) to be met at the door by the Bishop of Ripon and his registrar. The church was then consecrated.

The Bishop, in his sermon to a full church, commented on the contrast between the old and comparatively mean structure and the new, comely and beautiful edifice. The bells rang out.

Major Foster then hosted the luncheon at the school for up to 200 guests. Colonel Akroyd proposed 'The Bishop and Clergy of the Diocese' and reminded those present that the task ahead was to build the living stones of the congregation. The bishop, in his response, thanked Major Foster for his magnificent gift of the church and also commented positively on the possibility of the creation of a diocese in Halifax.

Major Foster responded by thanking those who had generously added their own offerings and praised the architect, clerk of works and everyone who had been involved in the building of the church. Mark Dawson proposed 'Church and State' to which Archdeacon Hey responded. The bells rang throughout the afternoon and evening. Rev Francis Musson, the Rector of Elland, preached in the evening and, on the following Sunday, the preachers were Rev W.P. Musgrave, Canon Residentiary of Hereford Cathedral, and Bishop Ryan. William Musgrave was a nephew of Archdeacon Charles Musgrave who had been the Vicar of Halifax for many years and a friend and supporter of St Matthew's.

St Matthew's was designated Grade II in December 1983 and the listing notes that the belfry tower at the north-west of the church is of four stages with the octagonal clasping turret a stage higher (it is over 90 feet high). Embattled parapets, gables feature strongly and the nave continues the Gothic Revival theme.

The nave is 71 feet long and 22 feet wide whilst the aisles add a further 11 feet on both sides. The chancel is 32 feet long and 19 feet wide. At the apex of the nave, the height is 38 feet. The church had seating for between 550 and 600.

On the north-eastern external wall are the arms of The Bishop of Ripon and Archdeacon Musgrave, Vicar of Halifax at the time the church was being built. The sculpture over the north door is of St Matthew, the patron saint, and that of St Cecilia, the patron saint of music, features on the choir vestry wall. We know that St Cecilia was carved by Signor Fucigua, an assistant to J. Birnie Philip.

Permission was granted in 1899 to extend the choir vestry by several feet providing the work did not interrupt divine service. Though the north face looks unchanged, there is evidence on the eastern faces of some alterations.

On the pediment over the door on the south side, next to the Foster Chapel, is a representation of the coats of arms of the Foster and Stansfeld families together with the motto *Justum perficito nihil timeto* – 'Act justly and fear nothing'. This side door would give access to the church for the family from their home at Cliffe Hill.

The octagonal gate piers are beautifully designed and carved forming an imposing entrance to the church's grounds. They are Grade II listed in their own right.

The new St Matthew's was provided with its clock by Sir Henry William Ripley M.P. It was electrified in 1970 though initially it was powered by a weight of around a ton. The clock face has a diameter of nearly five feet and the time is rung on six bells to the Cambridge chimes. The faces are set away from the wall of the tower. On a sunny late morning the clock face forms a beautiful shadow on the east side.

The original peel of eight bells was cast by Mears & Stainbeck and recast in 1970 in smaller moulds. The tenor bell weighed 18cwt (over 900kg) and was donated by the first vicar, Rev George Bagot, the seventh by Alice Sophia Sutherland Walker, the sixth by Alderman Mark Dawson, the fifth by Edward, Fred, Henry (Harry) and Hugh Ripley and the other three by members of the congregation by subscription. The first three had personal inscriptions on them.

The pulpit, font and reredos (an ornamental screen at the back of the altar) are all carved in Caen stone. The pulpit was given by Sir Titus Salt and the reredos by Mrs William Foster (Mary Ellen) of Hornby Castle. The latter is a low relief of *The Last Supper* from the studios of J. Birnie Philip – a sculptor of some note who worked closely with George Gilbert Scott, including at All Souls Church, Haley Hill and on the associated statue of Edward Akroyd. One account of the church also attributes the pulpit to Birnie Philip but this does not occur in other accounts. However, whoever created the pulpit was a superb craftsman as it is an excellent example of this form of sculpture. There is intricate detail carved into the panels and the balustrade. The handrail is red marble.

The elegant brass eagle lectern was donated by Abraham Briggs Foster of Northowram Hall. Immediately behind the lectern and low down is the brass dedication plate placed for Hannah Jane Foster which also includes the names of George Bagot, as vicar, Swinden Barber, architect, and the churchwardens, Joseph Thomson and Abraham Turner.

The octagonal font was given by John Foster junior of Holroyd House, Priestley Green and was carved in Caen stone by John Thompson junior of Peterborough. He was a well-known mason working in cathedrals, churches and secular buildings across the country. The main panels carry the symbols of the evangelists – a winged bull or calf for St Luke, a winged lion for St Mark, an angel with a scroll for St Matthew and the eagle for St John and these alternate with carved roses. The finials to the small arches are representations of masks and the faces of saints.

The massive wooden tower-like cover for the font, which certainly complements the fine carving of the font itself, was carved by James Christie of Huddersfield. The attribution in the centenary booklet to a James Clinsty appears to be based on a mistake in one newspaper's account of the consecration of the church. We could find no reference to a James Clinsty; in fact that surname is very rare indeed. However, there was a noted joiner in Huddersfield called James Christie who had worked with Swinden Barber on both St Peter's and St Paul's in Huddersfield and one newspaper account has James Christie as the joiner on the project. Around the base of the cover is carved a dedication to the founder of the church.

The baptistry window on the left is dedicated to Rev George Bagot, the first vicar, as is the central window of Christ teaching the children. The right-hand window is in memory of William Simpson Baines of Elm Royd, Lightcliffe.

The capitals and other stone carvings in the nave are by Charles Mawer of Leeds and depict the heads of saints and martyrs. The heavily timbered roof has an interesting alternating ogee arch design. Though now mainly covered in carpet, the floors are tiled. The patterns become more elaborate as one moves from the nave to the chancel and then the altar. These were supplied by Minton, Hollins & Co. of Stoke. The communion table rests on a piece of black marble.

On the north side of the chancel wall is a memorial plaque to Harold Lancaster Taylor MA, vicar here from 1914 to 1955. He was also an Honorary Canon at Wakefield Cathedral from 1936 until his death. His ashes lie beneath the chancel. To the left of the reredos you can read the Creed, the first four Commandments and the expectations for the keeping of the Sabbath; to the right, the Lord's Prayer and the remaining Commandments. On the south wall, there is a piscina, aumbry and credence shelf (used during the communion service) and a pair of gothic style headed sedilia where two celebrants can sit during parts of the service. In the choir there are nine brass plaques commemorating former choristers and an organist. Looking up, the brackets show angels carrying shields with instruments from the betrayal and crucifixion of Christ. These are attributed to J. Birnie Philip's studio.

The east window depicts the crucifixion and has a dedication to Samuel Briggs Foster and Alfred Foster. The West window given by William Foster of Harrobin's House, Queensbury contains two complete pictures – the visions of Ezekiel and of John. The clerestory windows, four pairs on the south side and three on the north, have stained glass depictions of Old Testament characters including Adam and Eve, Abraham, Rebekah, Rachel, David, Solomon and the Queen of Sheba.

The organ, built by Kirkland of Wakefield, was a gift from Evan Charles Sutherland Walker. It was not successful and was sold for £60 in 1903 when a new one designed by Gordon Salt and built in the City Organ Works in Bradford was installed. The cost was £1,350 and included the blower house which was in the south-east corner of the grounds. This was demolished in 2017. The organ had 2,381 pneumatic tubes and 25,000 feet (7,600 metres) of piping. This organ needed repairing as early as 1924 and was reconstructed at a cost of £1,500. The first organist was William Cook, headmaster of the National Boys School.

The Communion Table was given by Sarah Walton to whom a window, depicting Faith, Hope and Charity, is dedicated in the South aisle. There is a grand brass communion rail which originally had brass gas lighting standards at each end. A communion set of chalice, flagon and paten was given by Mr and Mrs Thomas Bottomley of The Grange in 1875. A silver mace was given by Mr and Mrs Sydney Norris. Another example of the generosity of the Foster family, as Mrs Norris was formerly Jane Foster, one of Jonas's sisters.

Few items came from the old church other than some altar plate. There are two chalices, one dedicated to Rev Richard Sutcliffe by his widow Martha 1782 and a much earlier one, hallmarked 1570, London, which may be the only connection between the original chapel and the new church. There were also a paten and flagon dated from 1823.

The Royal Coat of Arms which now hangs on the north wall originally hung on the gallery in front of the organ in the old church. It is relatively rare as it includes the arms of the Dukes of Saxony as it was assumed that, on Queen Victoria's marriage to Albert, it would be added. The Queen had different ideas.

Just inside the north entrance is a window, the work of Heaton, Butler & Bayne, dedicated to Emily Smith the daughter of J Senior. A wooden board, given in memory of Jennifer Brooke, lists the incumbents from Edward Hoppay in 1536 to the present day. There is a brass plaque commemorating Lumb Stocks and his wife Ellen. Lumb was a renowned engraver who had lived locally at Gawbert Hall and on Till Carr Lane before making his name in London. He was a member of the Royal Academy.

The Foster Chapel is to the south of the chancel and bears the family arms of the Fosters and the Stansfelds. There are brass plaques to Major Johnston Jonas Foster and to his daughter, Katharine Laetitia and, also, a marble tablet bearing similar dedications and adding Hannah Jane, his widow. The plaque reads

In Loving Memory of Johnston Jonas Foster,
Major of 6th West York Yeomanry Cavalry,
of Moor Park, Ludlow, Salop, and of
Cliffe Hill, in this parish, the Founder of this
Church, who died at Cannes in France.
February 26th A D 1880, aged 53 years.
His body rests in the vault beneath this Chapel.

The vault is alongside the south-eastern corner of the church. His widow, Hannah Jane (née Stansfeld), moved permanently to Richard's Castle soon after his death. There are two windows in dedication to the family including the Resurrection and Virgin and Child.

The Lady Chapel, created in 1925, was dedicated to the Glory of God and in memory of George Watkinson and his son Samuel Lord Watkinson both of whom were churchwardens and benefactors of the church. Samuel's brother, George, became the first vicar of Northowram and the family funded the building of St Matthew's church there. This chapel was on the south side opposite to the main door separated by screens from the nave. There is a carved dedication to the donors from their family in the top left panel of the

screen which now separates the nave from the entrance space. To the side of the altar is a window, depicting Mary, Joseph and the baby Jesus, dedicated to the memory of Sarah Scholes who died in 1869.

The carving of the chapel and that of the wardens' stalls that were originally below the west window are the work of celebrated local carver Harry Percy Jackson of Coley. In all probability the carvings were erected by Harry Gough, a joiner, who had his workshop at nearby Knowl Top. Jackson's son carved a bench dedicated to the memory of Canon Taylor and this would have been at the rear of the chapel and remains in the St Aidan's room.

In 1976, there was a major re-ordering of the west end of the church. The nave was terminated at the final pillars to create a social area. A doorway was introduced into the wall facing the main entrance, a partition created across the nave using both the carved panels from the wardens' stalls and the tracery carving from the Lady Chapel. This is interesting because you can see how the altar screen has been turned to face the east, the small shields that were above the altar are now seen from the end of the nave.

The heavier panelling with the crucifix above separates the nave from the social space and the war memorial has been moved to the south of a new doorway. This is balanced by the memorial, also by Jackson, from St Aidan's on the north. The altar table from the Lady Chapel is still in use in the St Aidan's room just a short distance from its original position. Later still a community area, called the Nyamatare Room after the parish's links in Uganda, was created adjoining the west end.

There was a mission church on Bradford Road at Bailiff Bridge opened around 1884 and dedicated to St Aidan. It closed in 1976. The pulpit was carved by H.P. Jackson. A Sunday School operated during its lifetime and, for a period of time, the Bailiffe Bridge British School was based there.

The photograph shows the church in the middle of the frame. It must date from pre-WWI, there are no tramlines. It was later used as a carpet warehouse by T.F. Firth & Sons. The memorial remembering those who fell in World War I was moved to St Matthew's Church in 1980. It is the one with the castellated top. This church is remembered by a blue and gold lettered board just inside the porch. The building still stands in 2020.

The first vicarage, now Abbotsford, was built on Wakefield Road opposite to what is now The Stray. The second (pictured right), built in 1900 on part of the Cliffe Hill estate and designed by J.F. Walsh, is a superb example of the 'Arts and Craft' movement. It was funded by a loan of £100 from the Queen Anne Bounty charity 'to build a parsonage house and office on the glebe belonging to the benefice.' The current vicarage is opposite the church.

The churchyard

From the time that the original chapel was built until around 1867 the churchyard would have been much smaller. It extended about 20 yards to the north of the church and was surrounded by farmers' fields. Of these farms three would have been at Till Carr, the Pear Tree and Mortimer's Farm, what is now the Sun Inn. This latter was then a coaching inn when the turnpike opened. What is now King George V Park had also been a quarry for a period of time. There were stocks at the south-west corner of the churchyard alongside Wakefield Road. These are shown on one old plan kept in the vestry and referred to by Horsfall Turner around 1900 as having been removed "in living memory". There is a burial near the spot dated 1826 so perhaps they had gone by then. Horsfall Turner writes that a silver triumphal coin of L Scipio Asiaticus was dug up in the churchyard in 1833 and that a Roman vessel and coins had been found in a neighbouring field between 1828 and 1823.

It was traditional that churchyards had a yew tree and one was recorded in 1764. There is no sign of it now but two yews have recently been planted to continue the tradition.

The cottage, known as the Priest's House or Curate's House dates from 1637 and stood to the north-west of the church. It was moved in 1866 by Evan Charles and Alice Sutherland Walker to its current site as indicated by a stone plaque high on its west wall. In the Lightcliffe Terrier (an inventory of church property) of 1764 it was described as a parsonage of two low stone-floored rooms with two chambers above.

The local names imply that it was lived in by the clergy and this was certainly the case in the early years. However, from the time this church was built the curates lived elsewhere. Richard Sutcliffe was Master at Hipperholme Grammar School and Robert Wilkinson was Headmaster at Heath Grammar School and they lived in houses at the schools. William Gurney lived locally in rented accommodation. These priests, and those before them, had a permanent position for life and were perpetual curates within the Halifax Parish. Lightcliffe became a chapelry in 1846 and a parish in its own right in 1869. The house was used by vergers or sextons. A responsibility of the tenants was to wind the clock. When the verger Francis William Bradley and his wife Fanny lived there they described the cottage as being 'cold and damp'.

Part of the salary of these curates was provided by the income generated by farms which had been purchased under the Queen Anne's Bounty scheme. 'The Act for making more effectual her late majesties [sic] Intention for augmenting the Maintenance of Poor Clergy' was enacted in 1714. It was a means-tested lottery purchasing land which provided an annual income for the curate. Lightcliffe benefited from four grants between 1749 and 1791. At least three farms were bought at Barley Croft, Blackshaw Head, Oatsroyd, and Sheard Green in Hove Edge. This latter was between Upper Green Lane and Finkil Street diagonally opposite to Nether House.

Although the churchyard was not authorised for burials until 1680 (by Dr Richard Sterne, Archbishop of York), the first burials that we have evidence for are from 1674. R. Bretton cites a deed of 1594 which has a cemetery attached to the chapel and Horsfall Turner says that the earliest burial, a person called Batley, was buried in 1665 and that this grave was found when the curate's house was moved. There is no firm evidence for this and the dates do not match.

The licence was granted because of the difficulty and steepness of the roads both for the infants and the bodies of the dead being carried into Halifax. Prior to that burials would have taken place in Halifax as would marriages. The early burials took place around the church and the boundary walls but only as far back as 20 yards beyond the tower. The churchyard was twice extended significantly, firstly in 1867 and then in 1934.

In the early days many churchyards were of approximately one acre – God's Acre. Ours was initially smaller but is now around 2.2 acres (1 hectare). The oldest known burials are off the pathway leading to the church with the most sought after being close to the church as possible.

The burial records until around 1812 are very difficult to read and contain only basic information such as name and date of death. Rarely is an age recorded nor where they lived. This means that more information is only available if there is still a memorial stone, usually a flat ledger grave marker or, if we have not yet found the grave, what was recorded by Arthur Blackburn around 1930. Burials before 1704 are not recorded.

Arthur Blackburn, from Wibsey, visited many cemeteries in the area and recorded the inscriptions on the memorials. In our case close to 1000, most of which, apart from some spellings, are accurate. His register is held in the church and proved of great value as the churchyard was being restored and recorded from 2012 to 2018.

From 1867 in the 'new' churchyard, every burial in the records included a plot reference based on a grid laid out when the churchyard was extended. Prior to that, no such reference is available. We can only know where somebody was buried if there is a permanent memorial.

What we do know is that the number of recorded burials increases from 163 in the decade 1710 to 1719 to 476 during 1810 to 1819. The first burials that have been found are those of Esther and Judith Hanson. Esther was from Hove Edge. There had been 11 marked graves by 1700. Others would have been buried but without permanent memorials.

In the years leading up to a series of Burial Acts from 1852 to 1885 there had been growing concerns nationally about the overcrowding of burial grounds with graves overfull and many close to the surface, so close that corpses could be seen in some churchyards soon after burial. There was mounting evidence regarding health issues, which would presumably apply to this churchyard as anywhere else in the country.

Up until 1867, when St Matthew's churchyard was extended, the area available for burials was approximately 1100 plots. Of these, 100 possible plots were to the immediate north of the church. Until around 1780 there was a superstition and tradition that it was inappropriate to be buried here. Only suicides and a few paupers would have been buried in this section. Horsfall Turner quotes a Mr Scratchard, writing around 1830, as saying that up to 50 years ago there was not one grave in the north side of the chapel and the first person buried there was a woman who destroyed herself. Certainly, that area would have been used by the village for fairs and games. There is no evidence of burials in this part of our churchyard until after 1832.

We know that in this 200-year period around 6,200 people were buried. Roughly speaking this implies the average number of burials in a plot would be between 6 and 7. Of course many of these would have been small children and, by the end of the period, early burials would have been completely decomposed. However, this still implies that a lot of burial plots were very full.

The burial records for many poor people and children indicate an area rather than specific plots. The entry simply says 'East'. It is likely that this was between the first Till Carr Lane entrance and the cottage. The headstones that can be seen there now date from 1940. Some infants, without a family grave, were buried in a recently dug grave with no family connection. Parishes had a coffin for common use which was emptied of the body at the time of burial and then reused – an early example of recycling.

Very few people were buried under the church itself; these include some priests. We have records of several curates and a priest from the south coast who died on a visit to the area. Local church benefactors such as the Holmes and Walkers were also buried under the nave. Most, if not all, would have been remembered either by a wall memorial or a brass plaque. Some of these are preserved either in the tower or the new church vestry. This form of burial became forbidden after the Burial Acts came into force. Where burials were allowed in other churches nationally very strict regulations had to be followed. We have no record of any burial under the church after that of Ann Walker in 1854.

When the extension was consecrated, the older part of the churchyard was 'closed' and only burials in family graves with remaining space were permitted. This Order in Council passed the responsibility of maintaining this part to the Privy Council which, in turn, passed it on to local authorities. This is why, although the Parochial Church Council has a legal responsibility to maintain the graves, Calderdale Council cuts the grass. There is a letter from the Council's Chief Administrative Officer to the vicar confirming this in 1977.

Regulations had been put in place in 1851 to maximise the use of the original churchyard by discouraging vaults and railings. Later regulations included a minimum depth for the first burial in a plot (nine feet) and the final burial to be at least four feet from the surface. A scale of fees showed that those from outside the parish were charged three times that of locals (£6 6s 0d rather than £2 2s 0d). These regulations were published in 1867 and signed by the incumbent, Rev William Gurney, the churchwardens, and Charles Musgrave, Vicar of Halifax. This latter indicates that Lightcliffe was still a chapelry rather than a parish.

Plans were put forward in 1932 to increase the burial area from the low wall to the rear of the current churchyard. They needed approval at government level, and this was granted by the Ministry of Health in 1932. In 1933 the land was purchased from Colonel Aykroyd with a plan for around 650 plots. Interestingly there was some concern then, as now, about the adequacy of the drainage. The price for the purchase was £278 10s with a further £285 for preparation including walling and planting and this was raised through an appeal. There is a list of the donors including Col Goldthorp, Dr Brown, Dr Lawson, Mr Watkinson and Mr Hellewell. The extension was consecrated by the Bishop of Wakefield in 1934. The first burials, however, were not until 1948.

In 1935 Major Alic Sutherland and Marion Gee gave permission for the plot of land originally given by E.C. Sutherland Walker to be merged into the new burial ground. This plot was for the burial of the infant William Sutherland Walker who died in August 1861 and, as a term of the gift of land, was to be maintained by the church in perpetuity. The large plot of 129 sq. yards lies to the north of George Mackay Sutherland's tomb, but there is no sign of a memorial to the infant William nor is there any evidence of the plot being used since this permission was granted. We do know that Arthur Blackburn did try to record an inscription which had part of the parents' names and no more, suggesting that it was heavily eroded by 1930.

At least one chest tomb, belonging to the Tate family, was removed, probably in the 1960s in an unofficial agreement between the vicar and the Parks Department to ease grass cutting. We have a photograph of this tomb next to the western doorway into the church taken in the 1920s. It was not on photographs taken in the mid-1960s. There is now just a piece of grass marking where the chest tomb was. There are other graves in the form of a large slab with a raised central rectangle in the middle. These were probably chest tombs.

After the demolition of the old church a proposal was put forward in 1973 to change the look of this part of the churchyard by forming rose gardens and increasing the grass area. This would have involved moving many ledger stones and tombs from around the old church site. However, the funding was not forthcoming and the project was not started.

In the mid-1980s a good number of headstones and memorials were laid flat in the name of health and safety. There is no evidence in the archives that diocesan approval was sought for this action. Many were placed face down resulting in their inscriptions being hidden from view. Some of this thoughtlessness has been put right either by re-erecting the headstones or turning them on to their backs so that they are again readable. Most headstones are remarkably stable and can lean at quite an angle and still be safe. There are regular safety inspections by Calderdale Council experts.

Of the 11,300 individuals buried in the churchyard we know little about the majority, other than what was written in the parish register e.g. their name, date of burial and sometimes the date of death and age. For children and wives, the name of the father or husband was sometimes recorded. And for some plots the owner, often a family member, was also noted. The memorial inscriptions on headstones, where they exist, give more valuable information such as family relationships and abodes.

Others we know considerably more about, mainly because they or their families were well known in the locality. In some cases, the Friends have researched in considerable detail the family stories, and these are published on the website. This began with a project to mark those who died in WWI to coincide with its centenary and has since extended to include others buried here or associated with the church.

The churchyard is a Commonwealth War Graves Commission site with four Portland stone memorials. These are visited by Commission staff every two years and are cared for by the Church and The Friends. A few more memorials are under the care of the Commission where a soldier who died from wounds was buried in a family plot. There are other family headstones which commemorate the dead of WWI who were buried where they died in Belgium, France and Africa. The family stories of all of these soldiers, and of May Hartley, the only female named on the Roll of Honour in the church, are published on the churchyard website.

The number of burials here and in other cemeteries, both faith-based and secular, has declined significantly over the years. From a peak of 780 per year around 1890s the number of burials began a sharp decline so that by the 1950s it was down to 220 and this trend has continued. There are now just a few buried each year. The decline is due, of course, to the increasing popularity of cremations which became legal in 1884. By 2016 over 75% of all bodies were cremated. A consequence is the unfortunate loss of a piece of social history. Cremated ashes are buried in a consecrated part of the grounds of the new church.

Over its history there have been times when the area was not looked after – back in 1902 there was an official letter of complaint about its state. The churchyard looked tidy in photographs in the 1970s but had become badly overgrown by the turn of the century. A voluntary group, Friends of St Matthew's Churchyard, was set up by Angela Monaghan in 2012 to restore the churchyard and to make it a place of respect for the dead, and a pleasant place for the community and wildlife. With financial help from the Heritage Lottery Fund, the local Council and their own fundraising, the Friends were able not only to clear the churchyard but to record all of the known burials. Some of the gravestones were just below the surface and found by careful use of a spade. A further six were found during the drought of 2016 by drone photography where they showed up as a different colour from the surrounding grass.

Cross checking with Arthur Blackburn's original list there are around a dozen still not found all of which are in the closed part of the churchyard. Almost every square metre has been tested and we are reasonably confident that the memorials are no longer here. It can only be assumed that they, like the Tate's tomb, were removed in the 1970s.

It is now possible to do a burial search on the website using names and year of death and this is frequently being used by families trying to find where their ancestors were buried. In the chapters that follow we tell the stories of some of the families with connections to Lightcliffe and the churchyard. We drew an arbitrary timeline of around 1920. Stories that are not included and further details of those that are may be found on the website under 'People of Interest'.

2 The Church Founders

The Lightcliffe Walkers and the Crow Nest Estate

The Lightcliffe Walkers, who were related to the Walkers of Walterclough Hall, probably resided in the area from the early seventeenth century, initially occupying Lower Crow Nest. Some of them were churchwardens at Eastfield Chapel, which preceded St Matthew's old church. Eighteenth-century parish records reference the baptism of Walker children 'of Crow Nest'. And burial records note a Walker as being 'of Lidget, Halifax' and another as a 'gent of Lightcliffe'.

The eldest son of 'William Walker of Crow Nest' – there were many Williams! – William Walker (1713–1786) married firstly Mary Wainhouse and on her death Elizabeth Caygill, the daughter of another wealthy Halifax wool merchant. He used part of his wealth, as we have seen, to rebuild the church. Crow Nest mansion and grounds were totally transformed, and Cliff Hill was also rebuilt as this William Walker became one of the largest landowners in the Lightcliffe district.

His eldest son, William Walker (1749-1809), inherited the Lightcliffe estate on the death of his father in 1786. A year later this keen musician and liberal benefactor was responsible for getting a Schnetzler organ installed in the church. William, like his sisters, Mary and Ann, never married, but his siblings Elizabeth and John did. Elizabeth Walker married John Priestley in 1776. Their son William Priestley became an eminent local musician, antiquarian and literary gentleman who instigated the founding of Halifax Choral Society. He and his bachelor uncle were responsible for encouraging musical performances at Lightcliffe church. In his 1809 will William Walker of Crow Nest , 'a gentleman of the strictest integrity and honour', continued to support the poor of the parish with an annual endowment which is acknowledged on the benefactors' board which survives to this day in the tower.

William's younger brother John married Mary Edwards, daughter of John Edwards of Pye Nest, in 1795. They lived at Cliff Hill when they were first married. It was there that their eldest son William – the seventh and last! – was born in 1798 and then died there three weeks later. He was buried in what would become this Walker family's plot just outside the church his grandfather had built. The couple had four more children: Elizabeth, Mary who died in 1815, Ann and John.

On the death of his brother in 1809 John Walker (1753-1823) inherited the Walker estate and his family moved to Crow Nest. His spinster sisters, Mary and Ann, moved to Cliff Hill which was where Mary Walker (1747-1822) died. She was buried within the church her father had built. There is a small commemoration plaque to her which is now kept in the new church. A year later her brother John and his wife Mary Walker (1763-1823) died. They were buried with their two children in their family grave just outside the church.

Although both grandfather William Walker and father John Walker attempted to make very good provision in their wills for their daughters, the bulk of the extensive Walker estate passed down the male line, in this case to the surviving son, John Walker. Two relatives, William Priestley and Henry Lees Edwards, were put in place as trustees and guardians to protect the estate. It was made up of cash, shares (many in the canal system) together with the mansion at Crow Nest, Cliff Hill, substantial other houses such as Lidgate, farms, pubs, cottages, mineral rights in stone, coal and ironstone. Much of this was local including 700 acres between Hove Edge, Norwood Green, Bailiffe Bridge through Lightcliffe and Hipperholme. In addition, there were properties in Honley, Huddersfield, Halifax, Greetland, Stainland and the Shibden Valley. In today's money it was probably worth in excess of £25 million.

At the time of his mother's death John Walker junior – still under the age of majority – was due to go to Brasenose College, Oxford, which he proceeded to do although he never graduated. It was said that John Walker junior enjoyed his fortune, reputedly over £6000 a year. But being young and inexperienced he had little interest in running the estate. He and his sisters continued to live at Crow Nest where they welcomed visitors and occasionally gave balls; they also attended balls in Halifax.

In the summer of 1829, John Walker married Frances Esther Penfold. Fanny, as she was known, was the daughter of Rev Penfold of Sussex and a niece through marriage of Christopher Rawson, a member of another influential local family. They had met when she had come to Lightcliffe to be a companion for Aunt Ann Walker who was on her own at Cliffe Hill after the death of her sister, Mary. Following the nuptials in Sussex John and Fanny set off for a Grand Tour honeymoon in Italy. But on 19th January 1830 twenty-five-year-old John Walker died in Naples where he was buried.

It took a long time for this news to reach the Walker family and for a pregnant Fanny to return to England. Apparently, Ann Walker went down to Dover to meet her, the Walker family possibly being fearful that a child would inherit. But later in 1830, at her parents' home, she gave birth to a stillborn son. With no heir and no will – John Walker died intestate – matters were complicated. There was much reading and rereading of his father's and grandfather's wills and the terms of the marriage agreement. Records show that Fanny's brother, James Penfold, came north to be involved in the negotiations. Eventually Fanny was granted a 'widow share' which was at least £2 million in today's money. It partly consisted of an annuity of £300 per year from the Walker estate, a share of the disposable wealth and the £2,000 worth of shares in the Calder and Hebble Navigation company. Fanny Walker had a memorial to her husband erected on the southern wall in St Matthew's old church alongside one of the pulpits. It survives still, in two parts, and is now stored in the tower.

The death of their brother, John Walker (1804-1830), left sisters, Elizabeth Sutherland as she was by then, and Ann Walker as extremely wealthy co-heiresses to the Lightcliffe estate and other properties. Sister Elizabeth Walker had met Captain George Mackay Sutherland at a ball and married him in Halifax in 1828. They would spend much of their married life in Scotland on his Inverness estate where most of their children were born, although George Sackville Sutherland, at the time their eldest son, was baptised at St Matthew's old church in 1831, presumably on one of their stays at Crow Nest. The Sutherlands occasionally stayed at Crow Nest and, with Ann Walker senior residing at Cliff

Hill, this may explain why Ann Walker chose to live at Lidgate House. Ann corresponded regularly with her sister Elizabeth in Scotland and also went to stay with the family there.

It was when Ann Walker was living at Lidgate House that Anne Lister of Shibden Hall began to visit her, although they had met briefly some years before. The friendship flourished and in 1834 the couple took communion at Holy Trinity, Goodramgate, York as a sign to themselves that they were married. This would not have been recognised by either church or community. Ann Walker then moved permanently to Shibden Hall. Their unconventional relationship would have shocked local opinion.

In a diary entry Anne Lister notes that she asked the Rev Robert Wilkinson if a pew was available at St Matthew's Church, Lightcliffe for Ann and her to use rather than the Lister pews at St John's Church in Halifax. Other diary entries note their presence at Lightcliffe services, some of which were also attended by the Sutherlands, again presumably when they were staying at Crow Nest.

During this time Ann Walker appears to have run her inheritance efficiently, advised by Anne Lister and ably assisted by her land steward Samuel Washington. Accounts show a steady and substantial rental income and few untenanted properties, balanced by expenditure on maintenance. Continuing in the family tradition, Ann bought property in the area when it became available.

Anne Lister was always keen to travel beyond Shibden and even abroad. It was on their last trip together in Georgia, that Anne Lister died in September 1840 after being bitten by a tick. Ann Walker returned to live at Shibden Hall, having been left a life interest in the Shibden Hall estate. She was there with servants on census night 6th June 1841.

Throughout her life Ann Walker had suffered periods of depression. But following Anne Lister's death her mental health and behaviour, in the eyes of her contemporaries, became a cause of grave concern. Her sister and brother-in-law petitioned for a commission to enquire into her supposed lunacy. In 1843 Ann's health was considered by an Inquisition (it really was called that) and it declared her a lunatic. She went from Shibden Hall to a 'licenced [sic] house for the reception of insane persons' at Osbaldwick near York. As a lunatic Ann had to have others act for her in the management of her estate, properties, stocks and shares. She could not even change the will she had made which still named George Sackville Sutherland as her legal heir even though he had died.

The Inquisition named George Mackay Sutherland as 'The Committee' to be responsible for her property and Elizabeth for her personal care In order to do this, they had to reside locally and so moved from Scotland to be closer. For health reasons Elizabeth Sutherland (1801-1844) was taken to Surrey where she died of consumption in 1844. Her widower and family returned to Yorkshire to Shibden Hall where Ann Walker was once again residing. Her teenage niece Mary Sutherland (1830-1845) died and was buried with her Walker grandparents in Lightcliffe churchyard. George Mackay Sutherland (1798-1847) 'of Aberarder, Inverness' died at Shibden Hall in April 1847. He was also buried in St Matthew's churchyard but in a tombed plot near the west wall in the closed section. On his death he was replaced as 'The Committee' for his sister-in-law by John Rawson and Mrs Dyson.

October 1847 also saw the death of Ann Walker senior (1757-1847) of Cliff Hill, the house she had lived in for most of her ninety years. She was the youngest daughter of the church benefactor William Walker of Crow Nest who in his will left her well provided for. Like her older sister Mary Walker, she was buried – at a cost of £260 – in a vault within the church her father had built. Originally there was a wall-mounted memorial in the church to both these sisters, but it has not been found. There is, however, a small brass plaque which was attached to a pew on the central aisle near to where she was buried. It is now kept within the vestry of St Matthew's new church. The wealthy spinster left legacies for some of her Rawson and Priestley relatives as well as making provision for the children of her niece, Elizabeth Sutherland

After her aunt's death Ann Walker junior moved back to Cliffe Hill in January 1848. She was there when the 1851 census was taken with her old friend Lydia Fenton née Wilkinson, as her housekeeper. Lydia, the youngest daughter of the Lightcliffe curate, Robert Wilkinson, had known and been a friend of Ann Walker over a long period of time. In her later years Ann Walker's mental health had improved and she was said to be of a more settled state of mind. She would have continued to have had the same standard of living as she had had previously as this was guaranteed by the lunacy legislation and clearly shown by the very detailed accounts produced, for the Committee at the time of Sutherland's death in 1847, by Samuel Washington, her land steward. The records suggest that her care cost at least £110,000 per year in today's money. It was only the poor who suffered in asylums such as Bedlam.

Ann Walker (1803-1854) died at Cliffe Hill on 25th February 1854 possibly of a stroke. The Rev Charles Musgrave, the Vicar of Halifax, officiated at the funeral and wrote to a friend that he had, that day, 3rd March 1854, interred Ann in the same vault as her Aunt Mary. Her only surviving nephew inherited the Crow Nest estate on the condition that he added the name Walker to his own, thus becoming Evan Charles Sutherland Walker. In her will Ann left the annual sum of ten pounds to be distributed at Lightcliffe Chapel, on Christmas Day in every year, among the poor of the Township of Lightcliffe. She made this bequest as a substitution for a similar bequest made by her uncle William Walker.

Evan Charles Sutherland Walker married Alice Sophia Tudor in London early in 1859. They lived at the Crow Nest mansion. Their first-born, baby William Sutherland Walker, died there in 1861. He was buried in the churchyard but his grave and headstone have never been found. At least two of their other children were also born at Crow Nest as recorded on their Lightcliffe baptism records. Ten years or so after her death Evan Charles Sutherland Walker erected the plaque commemorating his aunt Ann and some of his young siblings, Ann's nephews, who had died in their infancy.

The pulpit that the plaque refers to was probably added over the Walker vault when E.C. Sutherland Walker had the church refurbished several years after Ann Walker died.

In memory of Ann Walker, of Cliffe Hill,
who was born May 20th 1803,
died February 25th 1854, and
is buried beneath the pulpit in this church;

and her niece Mary who died in 1846, aged 15,
and is buried in this churchyard; and of
her nephew George Sackville, who died in 1843 aged 12,
and John Walker, who died in 1836 aged one year,
and who are buried at Kirk Michael, Ross-shire,
children of George Mackay and Elizabeth Sutherland.
ECASW 1862

(ECASW
stands for Evan Charles & Alice Sutherland Walker.)

His aunt's legacy made Evan Charles a seriously wealthy man, having already inherited his father's properties in Scotland together with his mother's inheritance. Some of this wealth was used for the benefit of others. In 1858 he sold land in Greetland for the new parish church of St Thomas together with a burial ground. Shortly afterwards he funded the improvements within St Matthew's Church which have already been mentioned and in the mid-1860s he gave the land and paid for the National School at a cost of £5,000.

Then, strangely after such a major commitment to the area, he moved back to Aberarder and put the entire Crow Nest estate up for sale. In 1872, he bought the Skibo estate of 20,000 acres for £130,000 and set about improving the estate including building a new, grand stately home. Unfortunately, he then discovered something that he should have investigated before making the purchase. The previous owner had given many of the tenants their homes and thus the income from the estate was severely restricted. His debts mounted until he became bankrupt. He was given a small annuity, enough to rent a cottage in Inverness. In 1883 he and his then eldest son William Tudor Sutherland Walker dropped the name Walker by deed poll.

Back in Lightcliffe the remnants of the Crow Nest estate which had not previously sold were put on the market again. The money generated by this 1890 sale went towards the debts. In 1898 the Scottish born American industrialist and philanthropist, Andrew Carnegie, bought the Skibo estate for around £90,000. This sum also helped to pay off Evan Charles Sutherland's creditors.

In July 1913 Evan Charles Sutherland (1835-1913) died in London where he and his wife Alice had lived latterly in a small, rented flat. The large land portfolio that several generations of William Walkers had built up was dissipated by Evan Charles, through delusions of grandeur and a lack of financial and legal acumen, in less than 20 years.

The Fosters

Major Johnston Jonas Foster, the second son of John Foster of Black Dyke Mills, Queensbury, was born in 1827, one of twelve children. He and his wife were the primary patrons of the new St Matthew's Church.

His father, John Foster (1798-1879) had been a mill owner from the mid-1820s, originally employing hand weavers. He was a keen musician who founded and funded the eponymous brass band in 1835. Also, in 1835, he acquired the land on which to build Black Dyke Mills from his father-in-law and the mill grew massively over the next decades. It was a family firm with John's sons, including Jonas, helping to run and expand the business. There were major extensions during the 1840s and 1850s including a weaving shed with 300 looms, a combing shed, a spinning mill and dyeworks. In fact, the whole process of manufacture of cotton, alpaca, mohair and silk was possible in-house. The workforce exceeded 2,000 and the mill area was over 15 acres. The family owned 1,200 acres in and around Queensbury including its own coal mines. The firm exported all over the world. This family was very wealthy.

The extensive Foster family owned Prospect House, Littlemoor, and Harrowins House in Queensbury, and Northowram Hall. John Foster had bought Hornby Castle near Lancaster in 1861 and made significant alterations to it including making the keep habitable and extending the accommodation. It was lived in by John himself and Jonas's elder brother Colonel William Henry Foster. Around 1879 William Henry and his brothers funded major alterations to Hornby village church, including a new roof, floor and changes to the structure of the aisles.

Jonas Foster married Hannah Jane Stansfeld (1842-1918) and added her mother's maiden name, Johnston, to his. Hannah's parents, Colonel Robert Stansfeld and Hannah Laetitia, were from Sowerby and are buried in St Peter's Church in that village. Jonas and Hannah had three daughters. Eighteen-year-old Katharine Laetitia was buried in Shropshire in 1883 but remembered in the Foster Chapel. Ethel Jane married the 15th Lord Inchiquin in 1896. Her sister Gertrude Stansfeld Foster (1870-1948) married the 3rd Marquess of Normanby in 1903.

John Foster senior and then Jonas were tenants of E.C. Sutherland Walker at Cliffe Hill. Jonas bought the house at the auction in 1867 for £15,600. The house was remodelled and had the family armorial bearings on the frontage together with the motto *Justum perficito nihil timeto* – 'Act justly and fear nothing' – which is also the motto of the Black Dyke Brass Band. The entrance pillars on the Coach Road bear his initials, JJF, and the date 1867. He also bought Green House and land alongside. The house and cottages were demolished. The terrace still known as Greenhouses was built in 1868, followed by the 'new' St Matthew's Church in 1875.

Jonas was a Major in the West Yorkshire Yeoman Cavalry. The group was formed on 3rd August 1842 by local mill owners following the Plug Riots of 1842, further civil unrest, and demonstrations by the Chartists. Jonas was elected as one of the first members of the Hipperholme Local Board in 1869 (Mark Dawson, see below, was the Returning Officer) and was the Board's Chairman from its inauguration until 1874. The Board initially met in the Whitehall Inn before acquiring its own offices further along Leeds Road. Jonas died in Cannes in 1880 but was buried back in Lightcliffe in the vault alongside the Foster Chapel.

Hannah then moved permanently to Moor Park, Ludlow, Shropshire, close to Richard's Castle, and Cliffe Hill was leased to William Henry Aykroyd (later created a baronet) who took over T.F. Firth & Sons, the carpet company, from his uncle. The Aykroyds gave the Bailiffe Bridge War Memorial and grounds to the community in 1921 and, in 1922, a new pavilion, within sight of both St Matthew's churches, to Lightcliffe Cricket Club.

When Richard's Castle's local medieval church of St Bartholomew's was in need of repair or replacement, Major Foster offered to build a new church in the village just before he died. His widow fulfilled the promise. The church of All Saints is dedicated to Johnston Jonas Foster and his daughter Laetitia and there is a brass plaque to that effect. The renowned architect, Norman Shaw, designed it. Johnston Jonas Foster was also responsible, with his brothers, for the replacement church of St Hilda's in Egton, near Whitby. It may be unique in the history of the Anglican Church for one man to fund three replacement churches and for his wife to lay two foundation stones. Other members of the Foster family built churches in Canwell, Staffordshire and Brockhampton in Herefordshire.

Hannah Jane Foster died in 1918 and was buried in the Foster vault in Lightcliffe church. The service was conducted by the vicar, Rev J Taylor, and Rev the Marquess of Normanby, her son-in-law. Memorial services were later also held in St Matthew's Church for Ethel Jane (1867-1940) and her husband (1864-1929), Lady and Lord Inchiquin.

As an aside, Hannah is reported as buying a Stradivari violin in 1889 and giving it to her daughter Ethel Jane. The violin was subsequently known as The Lady Inchiquin Stradivari (dated 1711).

3 Vicars and Teachers

Some of the vicars buried in the churchyard were also schoolteachers but we also have a selection of other teachers.

The nineteenth-century historian Horsfall Turner states that Rev Joshua Hill (1661-1733) was buried under the church (in this case the earlier Eastfield Chapel) in 1733. But there is no record of him in the parish burial records. There is an Ancestry family tree which suggests that he was the son of a Bradford yeoman, born on 8th November 1661, and died in Lightcliffe on 11th June 1739 – disagreeing with Horsfall Turner. As no evidence has been found to corroborate any of this information, we shall move on to people who we know more about.

Rev George Braithwaite (1709-1780) was curate at Lightcliffe between 1746 and 1748 before moving to Rastrick. He had a chequered career, being reported upon by the Archdeacon in 1766 that he was neglecting to perform Divine Service in the Chapel, guilty of great profaneness and immorality in drinking to excess, playing cards in public houses and committing the crime of fornication with Mercy Lacey. She was a single woman and his housekeeper. For this sin Mercy had to perform public penance 'wearing a surplice and with her hair hanging long down her back'. This service was conducted by George Braithwaite himself. In his later years, George Braithwaite became a reformed character and was instrumental in the rebuilding of St Matthew's Church in Rastrick in his final years.

Rev Richard Sutcliffe (c.1723-1782) was the curate at Lightcliffe from 1750 until his death in March 1782 aged 59 Previously he had been curate in Southowram before being nominated for Lightcliffe by Dr Legh, Vicar of Halifax. On 1st November 1751 he married Martha Robinson at St Mary's Church, Woodkirk. They were both from Halifax. It was during this time that the old St Matthew's Church was built, replacing Eastfield Chapel, at the instigation of its principal donor William Walker of Crow Nest. As well as being the first curate of the old church he was also headmaster of Hipperholme Grammar School for twenty years. The headmasterships of many schools in those days were often held by members of the clergy. Being a curate was not always a full-time job. He was the first clergyman that we can be certain of to be buried within the old St Matthew's Church.

To be buried under the church itself follows a long tradition going back to the Middle Ages when priests and wealthy landowners would be granted this privilege. There was a belief that being buried within a church or as close as possible to it gave you a better place at the Last Judgement. Rev Richard Sutcliffe's memorial is written in ecclesiastical Latin which, in translation, says that

> he was a loving husband, a true friend & kind to the poor. In short, a true Christian.

In his will, he described his wife, Martha, as being 'the best of wives'. They had no children, and it was mainly his nephews and nieces who inherited. It was a sizeable fortune including cash, silver, and properties in Northowram, Hove Edge and in villages in the Upper Calder valley, and Cooper House and Warley Wood in Warley. He also gave James Milns (c.1720-1797) two guineas per year if he was still Richard's servant when he died. James certainly outlived his master, dying in 1797 and being buried close to the church.

After Richard Sutcliffe's death in 1782 Rev Robert Wilkinson (1752-1839) became the perpetual curate. He too, was a headmaster but of Heath School, Halifax where he and his family lived. In December 1821 he took the funeral service of a visiting vicar Rev John Phillips (c.1753-1821) of "Bognor Regis, Sussex". As a clergyman Rev Phillips was able to be buried within the church. For nearly fifty years Rev Wilkinson travelled to Lightcliffe on horseback attired latterly it is claimed "in the olden style with knee breeches and buckles". He gets a number of mentions in the diaries of Anne Lister of Shibden Hall when she comments on the length and appropriateness of his sermons. As he aged there were also comments about his leadership of his Halifax school where numbers had declined to a mere handful. Eighty-seven-year-old Robert Wilkinson died in late 1839 and was buried within Lightclifffe church. He was also remembered in Halifax where there is a large tablet in the northern wall of Halifax Minster opposite to the south door. On this tablet his wife, Sarah, whom he had married in 1782, is described as 'tantum non mater' by her pupils – almost a mother.

In her diaries Anne Lister also notes that sometimes the Lightcliffe church services, which she attended with Ann Walker, were taken by Rev Wilkinson's son-in-law, Rev George Fenton (1795-1843), Vicar of Royston. Lydia Wilkinson, the youngest Wilkinson daughter, had married George Fenton in 1833. Being just a few years older than Ann Walker it is not surprising that the two were friends. After Lydia was widowed, she was involved with the care of Ann Walker, ending up as her housekeeper at Cliffe Hill. Both Rev George Fenton, his widow Lydia (c.1796-1865) and her unmarried Wilkinson sisters were buried in the churchyard in nearby graves with matching lettering on the memorial inscriptions on their ledger stones.

Rev William Gurney (1796-1869) succeeded Robert Wilkinson in 1840 as the perpetual curate. He served the parish for 29 years, having been in the ministry for 50 years, earning a salary of £270 per annum at the time of his death. For some years before his death, he was described as being 'weakly' and he was losing his sight. But he was still performing his duties, officiating at several funerals in 1869 before he died on 28th August 1869.

The Venerable Archdeacon Musgrave of Halifax, who had presented a large bible to the church, took William Gurney's funeral service. By then the practice of being buried under a church had been made illegal on health grounds. This explains why William and then, in 1881, his wife, were buried in the churchyard near the tower of the old church with this headstone. The Lightcliffe congregation erected a tablet on the east wall to William Gurney's memory but this is now lost.

The spinster Sarah Walton (1812-1887) was almost certainly one of Rev Gurney's parishioners. She was the daughter of a Halifax grocer who died when she was in her twenties. At the time of the 1841 census Sarah Walton lived with her cousin James Walton and his family in Sowerby Bridge where she was the children's governess. James Walton would go on to be a very wealthy man whose family business started the linoleum floor-cloth industry and Lincrusta-Walton wall decoration.

Sarah Walton ran a girls' school at Yew Cottage, Hipperholme, as recorded on the 1851 and 1861 census returns. Amongst her pupils were some of her cousin's children who she had been governess to years before. In an 1854 Leeds & Bradford directory under 'Academies' she was listed as being at Yew Trees. She has not been found in the 1871 census but in 1881 she was a visitor in Devon with her cousin's wife, the mother of some of her pupils. Hers is an unusual cope style tomb.

Rev Thomas Cox (1823-1887) was a "Clergyman without Cure of Souls" as he was a schoolmaster and then a headmaster. When he retired from his 23-year tenure of the headmastership of Heath Grammar School he moved from the School House to a house in The Crescent, Hipperholme, with his second wife, Emma. They were both buried in the churchyard, Thomas in 1887 and Emma in 1902.

Meanwhile, starting in 1866, Evan Charles Sutherland Walker, who inherited the vast Crow Nest estate from his aunt Ann Walker, had had Lightcliffe School built

to consist of a boys' school and a girls' school with master's and mistress's houses.

In 1872 William Cook (1842-1890) became the head of Lightcliffe Boys' School, living with his wife and family in the schoolmaster's house. During this time he was also an organist at the church. He died prematurely, aged 48, from 'bronchitis and weak action of the heart' on 8th November 1890. Four days later he was buried in the churchyard.

The third headmistress of Lightcliffe Girls' School was a local girl, Janet Berry (1864-1949), who had attended the school herself as a pupil. There is a record of her being admitted to the school in February 1869 and an examination and attendance schedule for 1877. She remained at the school as a pupil-teacher before going to Oxford Diocesan Training College. Then, after teaching in Clapham Park, London she was appointed as headmistress at Lightcliffe in 1891. Unfortunately, just three years later, the schools were so short of money that it was decided to amalgamate the two single-sex schools into one mixed school and Janet Berry lost her job. After a spell of teaching in Czechoslovakia she was invited to return, as her own successor, when the amalgamated status was scrapped in 1898.

When Janet Berry died in April 1949 she was buried with her parents and brother in the churchyard. The memorial inscription on this Berry headstone also pays tribute to her two nephews who were killed in France in WWI.

Down the hill in Bailiffe Bridge there was an elementary school. In 1879 a young man from Grosmont near Whitby became a teacher and eventually headmaster there.

Dr Scales and staff, year unknown

Dr Middleton Scales (1859-1922), of Woodlands House, was highly thought of according to the *Brighouse Echo*, and there is still a plinth with his name on it just outside the school. Unfortunately, the whereabouts of his bust which sat on this plinth – former pupils remember it – is no longer known. One of his assistant teachers in the picture may have been his sister Mary Jane Scales (1853-1915). After a spell as a servant to Joshua Smithson and his wife at Lydgate House she became an assistant teacher. Brother and sister as well as their mother were buried in the churchyard.

Rev Savile Brinton Lewis Hall (1897-1928) was the son of a Halifax painter. He may have been named after Sir Savile Brinton Crossley, MP for Halifax and part of the carpet manufacturing Crossley family. The Hall family subsequently lived in Northowram and then Hipperholme. During WWI Lewis (as he seems to have been known) served with the Duke of Wellington's West Riding regiment but then also with the newly formed RAF. His military records have the words "pilot" and "air ship" on them and he appears to have spent some time stationed at Mullion, Plymouth, a major RNAS airship base. His ranks are recorded as Sergeant and Lieutenant. After the war he appears on the 1918/19 Hipperholme register of United Grand Lodge of England Freemasons as a 22-year-old 2nd Lieutenant from Halifax. Quite when he took holy orders is unknown but when he died on New Year's Day 1928, he was a "clerk" in Swinton, Lancashire. If his parents were still living in Hipperholme when he died this may well explain why he was brought back to Yorkshire for burial in the churchyard four days later.

4 Soldiers and a Sailor

General Joshua Guest (1660-1747)

The earliest chest tomb in the churchyard is dedicated to Mary Smith (c.1641-1729), mother of Lieutenant General Joshua Guest. Mary Smith lived at one stage in Spout House at the junction of St Giles Road and Spout House Lane where her son, Joshua, was born in 1660. Her parents, Samuel and Mary Guest, were from Northowram and Mary was baptised in Halifax. She died in Lidgate in September 1729. The memorial inscription reads:

Here is interred the body of Mary the mother of Colonel Guest of Lidgate in Lightcliffe
who departed this life the 10th day of September Anno Domini 1729 aged 88 years.
Also of Joshua ye son of ye above said who departed this life August 1750, aged 63years.
Also of Mary his wife who departed this life August ye 1761, aged 63 years.
Also of Sammy Smith the son of Joshua Smith of Hove Edge
who died the 20th of July 1777, aged 42years.

The date on this memorial inscription for 'Joshua ye son' does not agree with our parish records. It also seems strange for Mary to have two sons named Joshua. Perhaps this Joshua Smith was a grandson or a stepson. A Joshua Smith was buried at Lightcliffe on 15th June 1750. However, son Joshua Guest began his military career in 1685 and the first entry of his name in existing War Office records is February 1704, when he was appointed cornet in Captain Henry Hunt's troop of Colonel George Carpenter's dragoons. A cornet was the first-level commissioned rank, equivalent now to that of 2nd Lieutenant. Commissions were expensive to purchase and to join the troop at this initial rank would have cost £840 (£77,000 in today's money) in 1837. We know from the inscription on his mother's tomb that he was a colonel by 1729 (this would be the equivalent of a further £500,000). He was a brigadier general by the age of 75 and finally a lieutenant general at retirement. The purchasing of commissions continued in the Army until the 1870s. It was seen as a way to ensure loyalty (if an officer was convicted of cowardice or desertion, he would be cashiered and would lose his initial investment) and to guarantee that he could afford the life of an officer.

Somehow Joshua had become quite wealthy. As the inscription on Mary Smith's tomb emphasises that she is the mother of Colonel Guest, it may well be that he paid for the tomb. The fact that it was the first such tomb by at least 30 years and was surrounded by plainer ledger graves is an indication of wealth. The tomb inscription shows that Mary was living at Lidgate at the time of her death. This was probably one of the few substantial houses in the area.

The whole of Guest's service as a commissioned regimental officer was passed in Carpenter's, afterwards Honeywood's, afterwards Bland's dragoons (later the 3rd Hussars). The regiment was raised in 1685. It fought with distinction under King William in the Irish and Flanders campaigns.

Joshua was in Scotland in 1715-16, and commanded a party of dragoons which pursued and overthrew Jacobite fugitives at Perth in 1716. The Lockhart Papers give a story, claimed to be directly from Guest, relating to the period of the Spanish invasion of Scotland in 1719. At the time Guest was with two or three troops of dragoons quartered in Staffordshire or Warwickshire. There he is said to have received letters, signed by King George I, directing him in case of disorder 'to burn, shoot, or destroy without asking questions, for which and all that he should do contrary to the law in execution of these orders he thereby previously indemnified him'. The temper of the district was Jacobite, and Guest communicated the orders to leading gentry with an appeal to them to keep the peace. The district remained undisturbed.

The 1745 Rebellion

In 1745 Guest was retired on half-pay of a regimental lieutenant colonel. He became a lieutenant general the same year and was sent from London to replace Lieutenant-General Preston as deputy governor of Edinburgh Castle. Under his command were two regiments of dragoons (Gardiner's and Hamilton's) plus the Town Guard.

Upon learning of the landing of Charles Edward Stuart (Bonnie Prince Charlie) and the rallying of his Jacobite supporters, Guest was ordered to send ships to bring Sir John Cope and his troops from Inverness in the north to reinforce Edinburgh. However, Charles and his growing army approached the city before this could be done. Gardiner's Dragoons had fallen back before the rebels before joining with Hamilton's regiment near Edinburgh at Guest's suggestion to await Cope's reinforcements. In the face of the rapidly advancing Jacobite force the dragoons under Brigadier Thomas Fowke retired to Prestonpans. The Battle of Prestonpans was seen as a success for the Jacobites.

This left General Guest to hold Edinburgh Castle with a garrison of only 600 consisting mainly of the newly raised Edinburgh Regiment, remnants of the dispersed Town Guard and volunteers. Varying accounts are given of his conduct when Edinburgh was in the hands of the rebels. According to some he was offered and refused a bribe of £200,000 to surrender the castle. Others including Robert Chambers in his 'Memorials of Edinburgh,' who bases his assertions on 'information received from a member of the Preston family,' declare that Guest was a Jacobite at heart and that at the council of war held on the arrival of the fugitives from the battle of Prestonpans he proposed to surrender, as the garrison was too weak to defend the place if attacked, and that this proposal was successfully opposed by George Preston, who remained in the castle as a volunteer, and according to this version was the real defender of the stronghold. This version of the siege was not given credence by the government and his career suggests that he was totally loyal to the government and trusted by it.

The castle was successfully held by General Guest and his garrison during the time Edinburgh was occupied by the rebels, the defenders cannonading Prince Charles's followers at the review preceding their march into England. Prince Charles ordered a blockade of the castle from 29th September 1745 hoping to starve the Government force into submission. Guest ordered the castle artillery to fire on the besiegers, which caused casualties amongst civilian residents in the neighbourhood and damage to their property. The Jacobite blockade was accordingly lifted on 5th October and supplies to the castle resumed under an informal truce.

Preston, a veteran of eighty-seven, who, it is said, was wheeled round the guards and sentries in a chair every two hours during the hottest part of the blockade, went to his Scottish home unrewarded. Guest returned to London in a horse-litter, after the overthrow at the Battle of Culloden (16th April 1746), to receive the gratitude of the king and people.

Guest died at his lodgings, Brook Street, London, 14th October 1747 and was buried in the East cloister of Westminster Abbey, where a monument was erected to him by his widow. The inscription reads:

Sacred to those virtues that adorn a Christian and a soldier
this marble perpetuates the memory of
Lieutenant General JOSHUA GUEST
who closed a service of sixty years by faithfully defending
EDINBURGH CASTLE against the Rebells [sic], 1745.
His widow, who lies near him, caused this to be erected.

Crimean War

Samuel Sharp (1822-1854) was a soldier in Portsmouth on the 1851 census. He then served with the 7th Foot (Royal Fusiliers) in the Crimea. On Sunday 5th November 1854 he was killed in the Second Battle of Inkerman. His name is recorded on the Sharp family's ledger stone below that of his twin brother, Joseph.

The death of William Flather (1833-1855) is recorded on the Flather family memorial at Lightcliffe as occurring on 3rd March 1855 at Scutari, Turkey. However, records of British deaths at Scutari do not appear to include William Flather. But there is a Wilson Firth who died on the same date. A letter addressed to Henry Flather 'Father of the late Wilson Firth 11th Hussars' would appear to confirm that they were one and the same person. Wilson Firth – why did he chose that name? - enlisted with the 11th Hussars at Liverpool on 26th November 1853. The 11th Hussars took part in the Charge of the Light Brigade in 1854 at Balaclava where Private Wilson Firth was wounded. He was relocated to Scutari, quite possibly into one of the Scutari Military hospitals that Florence Nightingale and other British ladies worked in, where he died.

Lightcliffe born Joseph Naylor (1823-1901) enlisted with the 5th Dragoon Guards in 1846 being stationed with his regiment in various parts of England. When war broke out his regiment was sent to the Crimea as part of the Heavy Brigade landing at Eupatoria. He fought at the battles of Balaclava and Inkerman and took part in the long Siege of Sebastopol. Of the 250 men of the regiment who left England at the beginning of the war, he was one of only thirty that returned. He and fourteen others were the only ones to bring back the same horse they took out. His horse was called Magpie. His regiment had a sumptuous banquet in Edinburgh given by the city and, one presumes, a more modest reception at The Sun Inn, Lightcliffe. He was stationed for some years in Dublin. After his discharge in May 1871, he returned to Lightcliffe and worked as a gardener for Mr Ripley of Holme House. By the time he died on 10th January 1901 he had become a Lightcliffe legend and his funeral was quite an occasion. Yorkshire Dragoons and children from Lightcliffe National School attended as well as local dignitaries. His rather splendid headstone complete with carved sword was erected by his admirers. The inscription proudly states that he served for '24 years and 315 days'.

During the Light Brigade's charge to the Russian guns, the Heavy Brigade was stationed on a ridge overlooking the valley. So it is possible that Dragoon Naylor saw William Flather ride into battle. The odds must have been long that three young men from the tiny village of Lightcliffe would be fighting 2000 miles from home.

Midshipman Alfred Ripley RN (1852-1870)

Alfred Ripley was the 6th son in a family of eleven children whose parents were Henry William and Sarah Ripley who were living in Holme House in 1864. He served on HMS Royal Oak as a midshipman for 2½ years mainly with the Mediterranean Fleet. HMS Royal Oak, which had both sail and steam, was converted into an ironclad during her construction as a wooden ship of the line. She was classified as an armoured frigate. In early September 1970 Midshipman Alfred was transferred to HMS Captain. He and many others drowned four days later.

During the Crimean War the navy had successfully developed a turret gun operating from an inshore vessel for bombarding forts. Previously, with fixed guns, the boat had to be moved to change the direction of fire. With the turret gun designed by Captain Cowper Coles, the boat could remain in a position and the turret moved. After the war, public pressure was mounted to build a warship with similar guns. USS Monitor (1862) was a small steam-powered coastal warship with a turret gun which saw action during the American Civil War.

HMS Captain was a masted but also steam-powered ship designed and built by a private contractor against the wishes of the Navy Controller's department. The Captain was completed in April 1870 and capsized, because of design and construction errors that led to inadequate stability, in the Bay of Biscay off Cape Finisterre on 6th September 1870 with the loss of nearly 500 lives. Of the crew only about 27 survived, though different accounts have different numbers of survivors.

The image of the ship gives an indication of why it was unstable. The navy still did not have confidence to power a ship by steam alone, so sails remained. Turret guns could not be placed on the main deck as their line of fire would have damaged the masts and rigging. The experimental turret guns can be
seen pointing out of large openings just above the water line.

There are memorials to the crew in St Paul's Cathedral, Westminster Abbey, and St Anne's Church in Portsmouth. The conclusion of the 1870 Court Martial is engraved upon the Memorial to the loss of *HMS Captain*, in the north aisle of St Paul's Cathedral. It blames the shipbuilders for a grave departure from the original design and exonerates the captain, crew and designer.

There is a brass plaque in Westminster Abbey dedicated to Captain Hugh Burgoyne V.C. and a memorial stained-glass window dedicated to the captain, 49 officers and 402 men and boys who died. On the southern wall of Lightcliffe's old church there was a memorial subscribed for by Alfred's former *Royal Oak* colleagues. When the Ripley family moved to Shropshire, soon after the new St Matthew's Church was built, they requested the tablet be moved to St Mary's, Bedstone near Ludlow. The request letter is in the West Yorkshire Archives.

The Ripley family made a significant contribution to the new Lightcliffe church. Sir Henry William Ripley, 1st Baronet (1813-1882), was a British businessman, philanthropist and politician. He was a principal partner in Edward Ripley & Son, an important dyeing company based at Bowling Dyeworks, Bowling, established by his grandfather in about 1806.

He was active in local politics and sat as a town councillor for the Borough of Bradford. He was also a JP, chairman of the Chamber of Commerce and took an active role in founding and running the Yorkshire Penny Bank. In 1866 he commenced construction of Ripleyville, an estate of 'model houses' for the working classes. There would be similarities with Akroydon and Saltaire. In 1864, he entertained Lord Palmerston, the Prime Minister, at Holme House for three days.

From 1868 he was also active in national politics. He was returned to Parliament for Bradford as a Liberal but his election was overturned on petition in 1869. He was re-elected in 1874 as an Independent but was defeated in 1880 when he stood as a Conservative. In 1880 he was created a Baronet, of Rawdon in the County of York and Bedstone, Shropshire. He died in November 1882, aged 69, and was succeeded as second Baronet by his eldest son Edward.

Bedstone Court was built for Sir Henry Ripley but he died before it was completed. A "calendar" house – 365 windows, 7 entrances, 52 rooms and 12 chimneys. It is now an independent boarding school. Amongst many others, Sir Henry William would have known Sir Titus Salt as a neighbour in Lightcliffe and Alderman Mark Dawson, a fellow Bradford politician, who lived in Hipperholme and had a mill a mile or so from Ripley's dyeworks.

The two World Wars would claim the lives of some of his descendants. They are remembered under Midshipman Alfred Ripley's original memorial now in St Mary's Church, Bedstone, Ludlow.

The Great War

The war memorials in many towns and villages were inscribed with the names of the fallen from that locality. Down the hill at Bailiffe Bridge the names cover four sides of their memorial. But the war memorial on The Stray has no names on it. There are, however, two rolls of honour in the new St Matthew's Church; one having been moved there from St Aidan's chapel in Bailiffe Bridge. The names of most of the 24 WWI soldiers buried and / or commemorated in the churchyard can be found on at least one of these memorials. A brief pen picture of each one of them follows in the order that they fell.

By the commencement of the Great War Frank Newsome may already have been a reservist. Because, although he was a "Stone Mason" at home on 2nd April 1911, his enlistment date was given as 4th December 1903. His battalion, the 1st Northumberland Fusiliers, was stationed at Portsmouth on 4th August 1914 and then mobilised for war ten days later, landing at Le Havre on 14th August 1914 as part of the British Expeditionary Force. They were immediately engaged in various actions on the Western Front including the First Battle of Ypres in which he was killed on 11th November 1914. He is remembered on the Menin Gate at Ypres and on the family headstone in the churchyard.

As soon as he was able, young Fred Mitchell enlisted with the Prince Albert Guards spending most of his military service in South Africa. He was there throughout the Boer War and then with the Brand's Horse, 5th Regiment, in South Africa fighting under General Botha in the campaign against the Germans. The forty-four-year-old was killed in action on 1st July 1915 just before the fighting in Otavi ceased. Even though he probably had not seen his family in Bailiffe Bridge for some time he was remembered on the family headstone in Lightcliffe churchyard.

Joseph Alfred Holt is remembered on his grandfather's headstone in the churchyard. He and his mother were living with his grandfather John Wheelhouse at the time of the 1911 census, at which time his father was in hospital. Then in 1912 he married Mary Ann Cryer, they had no children. His grandfather passed away in 1913 and when WWI started Joseph signed up with the West Yorkshire regiment. He was killed in action on 31st October 1915.

Another Lightcliffe lad who signed up almost immediately WWI started was Roland Walker, one of the twin sons of Donald Walker, a manager at T.F. Firths & Sons. The Walker family lived at No 2 Grange Terrace almost opposite the new church. The Walker children would attend Lightcliffe National School with the boys then going on to Hipperholme Grammar School. After school Roland worked for Messrs. Wayman & Co., Haley Hill before joining the Duke of Wellington's West Riding Regiment in September 1914. On the night of 9th December 1915 Roland Walker was with a working party in the trenches in Flanders when he was hit in the chest by a bullet which killed him instantly. Two weeks later, on 23rd December, his father Donald Walker (1858-1915) collapsed at work and died shortly afterwards.

On 25th November 1915 Walter Pybus married Ivy Tordoff in Halifax. He was a "Jeweller" and she was a "Burnisher" for a "Jeweller" which was presumably how they met. Not long after that Walter enlisted with the Royal Flying Corps and was sent for training to Salisbury Plain. Within a month he had an attack of influenza, which developed into pneumonia, resulting in his death on 4th April 1916. His body was brought back to Lightcliffe for interment in the same grave as his grandmother and step grandfather, Hannah and John Smith.

Nearly two years after losing her eldest son, Mrs Georgina Newsome received the news that a second son, Charles Newsome, had died of wounds on the first day of the Battle of the Somme. He enlisted on 15th March 1915 and arrived in France the following New Year's Day. He was with the 'A' Battery, 164th Brigade, Royal Field Artillery (32nd Division) when he died on 1st July 1916. He was buried at the Bouzincourt Communal Cemetery Extension. A third brother, Frederick William Newsome, served and survived, whilst a fourth brother Joseph Richard Newsome worked on Halifax railways during the war.

As a child Edward Schofield had attended Lightcliffe National School. Later he married and had five children and moved to the Hoyle's Buildings in Halifax. Before the outbreak of war, he was a Halifax Territorial. On 1st June 1915 he enlisted with the West Yorkshire Regiment. They too were involved in the first days of the Battle of the Somme, when Edward sustained a very severe leg wound that turned gangrenous. Despite the efforts of surgeons who amputated his leg at No 26 General Hospital he died on 9th July 1916 at 5 o'clock in the evening. He has a Commonwealth War grave in Etaples Military Cemetery, France and is remembered on his grandfather's ledger stone in Lightcliffe churchyard.

Almost immediately war was declared Arthur Rushworth joined the West Yorkshire, 12th Battalion, which was formed in September 1914 as part of the Third New Army (K3). They were mobilised and landed at Le Havre in September 1915. Arthur had only been involved at the front for three weeks when he was killed in action on 17th August 1916 at the Somme. He is remembered on the Thiepval Memorial and on his parents' headstone. His half-brother George Rushworth served with the Royal Flying Corps and survived.

Christopher Kershaw joined the Brighouse Territorials in 1909 when he was employed by H. & J. Sugden's at their George Street Mill in Clifton. He went to the front in April 1915 and then returned a year later when he re-enlisted after his time with the Territorials expired. In the brief time he had on leave he married Annie Crowther on 15th April 1916, the day his records show him as having re-enlisted. On 2nd September 1916 he was buried in a dug-out along with six others. He was dead when they got him out. He is remembered on the Thiepval Memorial as well as on the family ledger stone in the churchyard.

In early 1916 Aaron Sucksmith must have been employed by the British Millerain Co., Halifax who had their appeal for his exemption from fighting dismissed in March. He joined the Durham Light Infantry in April 1916. After training in North Shields, he went out to France from where he wrote this letter.

Dear Mother and Sister just a few lines to let you know that I am alright yet, but we are going up into the firing line again in a day or two. We are having some very fair weather over here just now. Theirs [sic] a lad called Wormould in this Company. He told me he used to live in that old house under the Bridge about 8 years ago. The next time you send a parcel put some ointment in that will kill fleas as I have had a few on me just lately. Let me know how Jim and Walter are going on. So I think that is all at presant[sic].
From your Loving son Aaron. I am in the pink.

Ten weeks later his parents received the news that Aaron had been killed in action somewhere in France on 4th September 1916. Aaron Sucksmith is remembered on the Ploegsteert Memorial, Hainault, Belgium panel 8 and 9 as well as back home in St Matthew's Church, Lightcliffe. His brother Walter had left for the front just a fortnight before. Another brother James had been with the Grenadier Guards since 1914. He was currently serving in Salonica where he had been since October 1915. And a younger brother Leonard had just enlisted with the South Wales Borderers on 24th June 1916.

The Booth family lived at 7 East View, a stone's throw across King George V Park from the churchyard. From there two Booth sons would go to serve in WWI. The eldest, Fred Booth, was killed in the early morning of 26th October 1916 somewhere on the Somme when a shell caused the roof of his dug-out to collapse burying him. He was at once dug out but was already dead. His younger brother Donald only saw action in the later months of the war which he survived.

Hesketh Place, near to East View so again close to the churchyard, was the home of the Shaw family. The eldest son Joe Willie Shaw – one-time Secretary of Lightcliffe Cricket club – joined the forces in June 1915, at Halifax, and proceeded to Chatham for training with the Royal Engineers before being sent to France. He was in an engagement at Fricourt, where, on June 24th 1916, he received a dose of gas, and, after being taken into hospital at Rouen, he was transferred, on July 8, to the Woodlands Hospital, Southport, where he was frequently visited by his parents. Although his health improved after being moved to Southport he relapsed and died on 8th October 1916. His body was brought back to Lightcliffe for burial in the family grave plot after a funeral at St Matthew's new church where, as a boy, he sang in the choir.

The Sucksmith family of St Giles Road, Lightcliffe received more bad news just three months after losing their son Aaron. His brother Walter Sucksmith had joined the West Yorkshire regiment in February 1916 and after training at Clipstone went out to France in August 1916. He sustained a bullet wound to the chest from which he died on the 8th December 1916 at the 33rd Field Hospital. He was buried in the Mesnil communal cemetery extension. The Sucksmith family had lost two sons, had a third serving in Salonica and a fourth with the South Wales Borderers.

George Percy Stephenson Brown was a member of the Brown family who were Hipperholme Wesleyans. He trained as a schoolmaster and went to teach in Liverpool, where he lived with his wife and two young sons. After the second Military Service Act he signed up on 2nd May 1916 with the King's Liverpool Regiment and went to France in November 1916. He was killed in France on 26/27th September 1917. As one of 'the missing' his name appears on a panel in Tyne Cot as well as on the family headstone in the churchyard.

Before the Great War James Smallwood helped on the family farm, Roydlands Farm, Hipperholme, and with the running of a carting and cab business. He did apply for exemption because of these jobs but as the Brighouse Echo reported on 28th July 1916 his case was dismissed. Shortly afterwards he was conscripted into the Grenadier Guards. In February 1917 he went to France. He was killed in action on 1st August 1917 and buried at the Artillery Wood Cemetery, West Vlaanderen, Belgium. His name appears on the Roll of Honour at Lightcliffe Church and on his parents' headstone.

Arthur Naylor was the great great nephew of the Crimean soldier Dragoon Guard Joseph Naylor but unlike Joseph his military career was brief. He joined the colours early in 1917, and, after training at Canterbury, was drafted to France in the September. On 20th October he was wounded. He died on 11th December 1917 at the 4th General Hospital and was buried at Etaples Military Cemetery. He is remembered in the churchyard on the plot that his mother and stepfather Hannah and Law Broadley would eventually occupy.

Bachelor Herbert Pybus, the brother of Walter, had originally been exempt from service as he worked for his invalid father in the family grocery business. However, in December 1916 a tribunal refused further exemption, but to enable arrangements to be made for the carrying on of the business Herbert was not to be called up before 31st January 1917. He then served with the Grenadier Guards. Whilst repelling an enemy attack on 27th March 1918 he was killed in action. He is commemorated on the Arras Memorial, Pas de Calais, and on the family plot at Lightcliffe where his brother was buried.

Another 27th March 1918 Lightcliffe-commemorated casualty is Edgar Sharp, except the inscription on his family's headstone gives his death date as 24th March 1917. Was this an error or do we have the wrong chap? Army records have an Edgar Sharp of the 9th Battalion, Kings Royal Rifles Corps, dying of wounds on 27th March 1918 and no March 1917 record for an Edgar Sharp(e). Our conclusion is that the Edgar Sharp who died in 1918 is the soldier remembered in the churchyard as well as on panels 61-64 of the Pozières Memorial.

John Raymond Berry and his older brother Kenneth Raymond Berry are remembered on a family headstone where it says that they were both killed in France. Both were former Hipperholme Grammar School boys. Kenneth signed up first and won the Military Medal, but no death record has been found for him. John, who worked for L&NW Railway, had initially failed the eyesight test for the Inns of Court O.T.C., at Berkhampstead. He joined the Machine Gun Corps in 1916, going out to France on May 25th, 1917. He died of wounds aged 21, on April 26th, 1918 in the 30th General Hospital, France.

Although Joe Lumb Brook of the Royal Field Artillery survived the fighting in WWI, he did not survive the 1918 Influenza pandemic. On 24th December 1918 he died of pneumonia in a Barnsley Hospital whilst at home on leave. He was then brought back to St Matthew's churchyard for burial on 28th December 1918. A CWGC headstone marks his grave which is in front of his grandfather's headstone. His wife Clara left a moving tribute at the foot of the original wooden cross. We are pleased to see that family members, perhaps descendants of his son Joseph Lumb Ernest Brook, have recently found their ancestor now that the once overgrown churchyard has been cleared.

The Brownrigg family lived at 5 East View and were therefore near neighbours of the Booths. Robert Brownrigg joined the A.S.C. Motor Transport on November 9th, 1914 and, after training at Southport, Sevenoaks and Reading, he was drafted to France on October 1st, 1915. He passed through the whole period of the war without being wounded but his health suffered. On his return home he contracted influenza and then bronchial pneumonia. He died on 7th March 1919 and was buried in the churchyard.

The names of three Aspinalls, two of them brothers, head the alphabetical list on the Bailiffe Bridge memorial. Harry Aspinall was employed by Messrs. T.F. Firth & Sons at Bailiffe Bridge before enlisting with the "Chums" on 4th March 1916. In November 1917 he was wounded but had recovered well enough by June 1918 to return to active service overseas. He was killed in action on 24th October 1918. His older brother Milton Aspinall survived the war. But Army medical records show that he was hospitalised in March 1918 with a vascular disease of the heart. This condition most probably contributed to his early death aged 34 on 13th December 1919 back in Bailiffe Bridge. He was buried in the churchyard in a plot marked with a black marble cross.

From his British Army WW1 Medal Rolls Index Card Leonard Sucksmith, having enlisted with the South Wales Borderers, would seem to have been in a Lincolnshire Regiment and then a Monmouth Regiment and to have served oversees but it is not clear as to where. What is clear is that he was discharged on 12th August 1919 because he was "No longer physically fit for service". A family descendant has explained that this was a very severe leg wound which probably contributed to his death on 23rd November 1920. He was buried in St Matthew's churchyard with a CWGC headstone. Thankfully, brother James (Jim) Sucksmith survived. Having lost three sons, the Sucksmith family had suffered enough.

There is one female name on the WW1 Roll of Honour in St Matthew's new church. May Hartley (1888-1916) was born in Leeds in 1888 but soon afterwards her parents moved May and her many siblings to various addresses in Hipperholme-cum-Brighouse and Bailiffe Bridge, before finally ending up at 80 Wakefield Road. Her father, John Alfred Burnett Hartley (1860-1923), was a stuff presser/finisher. As a 12-year-old May and her 14-year-old sister, Ida worked as hands in a cotton card room. By 1911 most of the Hartley family worked at the Firth's carpet factory in Bailiffe Bridge. When WW1 broke out May became a munitions worker at Brooke's explosive works in Lightcliffe. On 28th November 1916, whilst working in a first-floor room, 28-year-old May stepped on a trap door of a hoist. The trap door, like others in the room, was supposed to be safe to walk on but this one swung open. May fell through the hole and hit her head on a rail ten to twelve feet below. She was knocked unconscious and died half an hour later. In the subsequent inquest the jury found death was due to an accidental fall and that there was no criminal damage. Three of May's brothers served in WW1 and survived. And her sister Ida served with the Queen Alexander Imperial Military Nursing Reserve, having been one of the first woman to qualify as a state registered nurse.

Families with more than one family member involved in the Great War is a recurring theme, as witnessed by the number of brothers remembered in the churchyard. Back home waiting for news – and letters such as the one Aaron Sucksmith wrote – must have been terrible for the rest of the family.

One of the anxious Lightcliffe mothers would be widow Georgina Newsome, née Brittlebank (1857-1930). She was not a native of Lightcliffe having been born at Sandhurst, Berkshire where her father was a Sergeant Major in the 6th Dragoon Guards. Later this large military family would move to Worcestershire. Meanwhile her future husband, William Pickard Newsome (1855-1901), a stone mason from Wyke, the son of a farmer/groom, had also, unusually for the time, travelled to Stourbridge, Worcestershire. In 1883 Georgina and William were married in the Brentford district of Middlesex which was where their eldest son was born. But then by 1885 they had moved back up north to Hipperholme. Georgina and William had six children, four sons and two daughters. William Pickard Newsome was in hospital on the night of the 1901 census and died shortly after. Then a year later Georgina lost her father. By 1911 one of Georgina's sisters, Blanche Brittlebank (1864-1943), was living with the family. And then the Great War started. Of the four Newsome brothers three signed up. Frank was killed in action in November 1914 and then two years later Charles died of wounds. This prompted the *Halifax Courier* to carry this picture of the four young men.

FOUR HALIFAX BROTHERS: TWO KILLED.

Pte. F. Newsome, 1st Northumberland Fusiliers, 1, Heathfield-grove, Heath Lane, Halifax. Killed Nov. 11, 1914.

Mr. Jas. Newsome, shunter at Halifax Station.

Lt. Fred Wm. Newsome 10th Northumberland Fusiliers, now in France, where he has been 11 months. He was employed at Hali-fax ...

Bomb. Chas. Newsome, R.F.A. Died from wounds received July 1

Pte. F. Newsome   Mr Joe Newsome   Lt/ Fred Wm Newsome   Bomb C. Newsome

Seven other members of this extended Brittlebank family also served in WWI. A nephew, Jack Butler, the son of another sister, Emily, was the third casualty killed in action in 1918.

The military calling in Georgina's family was probably something that she understood very well but having been widowed early and then losing two sons and a nephew she must have been relieved to have had another son at home and then overjoyed to get her fourth son back safe and sound. When Georgina died in 1930, she was buried with her husband in the churchyard and then her sister was interred there too in 1943.

Meanwhile, the Lightcliffe fallen were remembered in Memorial Services held at St Matthew's Church on Sunday November 3rd 1918:

> For the following Officers, Non-commissioned Officers, and Men from the Parish of Lightcliffe who have died for their country during the year:

The list of names includes most of those above and many more.

There were others involved in WWI who survived the war to lead normal lives again but who were eventually laid to rest in the churchyard.

One of these was career soldier Alfred Wood (1881-1948) who enlisted as an eighteen-year-old with the Royal Field Artillery. He was the eighth child of ten and one of the numerous grandchildren of Thomas Wood, a stone mason who built some houses named Hesketh Place near the churchyard. These were originally known as Wood's Buildings. During his twenty-one-year military career Alfred Wood served in India and South Africa as well as being involved in military training at barracks in Glasgow and Sheffield. Then, during active service in France in WWI, he was awarded the Military Medal for 'bravery in the field'. After the war he brought his wife and son back to the West Riding to Hove Edge from where he ran his own business, eventually retiring in 1935. He was an active public figure, sitting as a local councillor on many committees as well as being heavily involved with the Ebenezer Chapel at Bailiffe Bridge. During World War Two he was a Hove Edge Air Warden.

Alfred Wood's father-in-law, who also became his brother-in-law, was another long service soldier who was also stationed in India and Glasgow with the Royal Field Artillery. But unlike Alfred Wood he was not a Lightcliffe lad. William Boswall (1862-1938) was born in London's East End, the son of a 'Tripe Dresser'. His family fell on hard times with both his parents and his second wife spending time in East End workhouses. Perhaps to 'escape' from, by then, a very complicated family situation, the 'Bootmaker' enlisted at Great Yarmouth under the alias William West in 1894. But before his daughter married Alfred Wood, and then he married Alfred's older sister, he signed army documents declaring that his real name was William Boswall. During the early part of WWI Saddler Corporal William Boswall was stationed at Aldershot. His twenty-two-year military career ended in October 1916. At some point before his death in 1938 he and his wife, Alfred's sister, moved to one of the Hesketh Place houses her grandfather had built.

Another military man who survived the Great War, although he was too old to fight overseas, was Reginald John Sowerby (1854-1922) who along with his father ran the Halifax publishing house Milner & Company, founded by a Halifax grocer and merchant William Milner. In the 1870s and 1880s Reginald Sowerby volunteered with the 1st Volunteer Battalion, the Duke of Wellington's (West Riding Regiment). Then, during the Great War, he was involved in Halifax with recruitment for his old regiment. He and his wife Emma lived at Holly Bank, Bramley Lane, before settling at 5 Oak Mount, Sutherland Road, where both died.

World War Two

There is one CWGC headstone in the churchyard for a WW2 soldier, Stanley Alfred Albert Roff. He was a Wiltshire man from Marlborough who served as a sapper with the Royal Engineers. Late at night on 22nd June 1941 he and a fellow Sapper were walking along Wakefield Road by Lightcliffe church when they were struck by a van travelling in the same direction. Sapper Roff was killed outright but his comrade, although very seriously injured, survived after time in Halifax hospital. Stanley Roff's death certificate states that he was 'Accidently knocked down and killed by a Motor Van'. An inquest was held on 24th July 1941. Stanley Roff was buried in plot J30 on 27th June 1941 with this CWGC headstone. He is also remembered on the Roll of Honour at Burbage, Wiltshire and in Royal Engineer lists.

5 Some Crow Nest and Shibden Hall Tenants

The death announcement for James Washington (1755-1839) in the *Bradford Observer* 18th July 1839 states:

> In his 85th year James Washington of Lightcliffe near Halifax. He was a faithful servant, having acted for half a century as bookkeeper to the firm of the late Messrs William and John Walker, cloth merchants, Crow Nest

Birstall-baptised James Washingon moved to Hipperholme and then in 1783 he married Esther Mann. Members of the Mann family had burial plots at the front of the old church, covered by beautifully engraved ledger stones. A year after they married, James and Esther occupied a house owned by Mr William Walker of Crow Nest, Lightcliffe, the start of a long association between the Washingtons and the Lightcliffe landowning Walkers. Five children were born at this Crow Nest estate cottage, the youngest of whom was Samuel Washington (1797-1857). James Washington, eventually a land surveyor as well as a bookkeeper, must have encouraged his son Samuel to follow in his footsteps. Samuel Washington drew up a map of the local area in 1820.

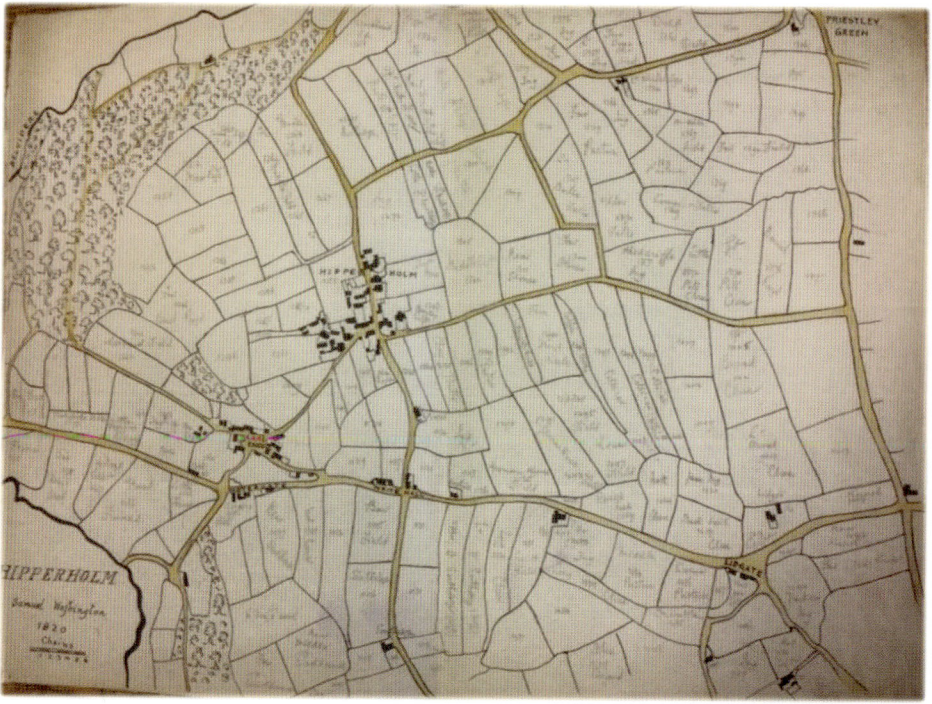

In 1822 Washington father and son's occupations as listed in *The History Directory & Gazetteer of the County of York, 1822, Vol I West Riding* were

> Jas Washington, surveyor of highways;
> Samuel Washington, schoolmaster & land surveyor

James Washington died on 7th July 1839 and his wife Esther Washington (1755-1842) on New Year's Day 1842. Both were buried in a Washington plot close to the five Mann ledger stones.

Before then, in 1824, Samuel Washington had married Hannah Cordingley. Their only son died as a baby, but their many daughters survived until at least their teenage years. All were baptised at St Matthew's Church, Samuel being described as either a "land surveyor" or a "land agent". This was after he became the Crow Nest land agent for the Walkers. At first, this Washington family lived at 'Helliwell' Syke, then Fenny Royd, then Crow Nest – perhaps in part of the main house or in one of the cottages, – and finally Lidgate House.

In 1832 Samuel Washington was asked by Anne Lister of Shibden Hall to become her land steward after the death of the previous steward John Briggs. In Anne Lister's later diaries there are many references to Anne Lister and Ann Walker consulting and meeting up with Samuel Washington about matters on their adjoining estates, although by the time the two of them departed for their European tour in 1839 Samuel Washington was only acting on Ann Walker's behalf for the Crow Nest estate.

Anne Lister died on this tour and Ann Walker returned to live at Shibden Hall where she was on 6th June 1841, the night of the census. Again, Samuel Washington was very much involved in the day-to-day running of the Crow Nest estate and then in the complicated dealings around Ann Walker's lunacy committal. There are several incredibly detailed documents in West Yorkshire Archives relating to Samuel Washington's work as the Crow Nest land agent. He was responsible for collecting the rents from tenants as well as managing repairs and other financial aspects.

Between 1843, when Ann Walker was declared a lunatic, and the death in 1847 of her brother-in-law George Mackay Sutherland, who was responsible for her financial affairs as 'the Committee', Samuel Washington drew up extensive accounts for the estate. The final one was 25 pages long and included the price when buying and selling properties through to incidental expenses such as the cost of providing refreshments for the workers. His work must have involved a great deal of travel around the immediate area and also to the outlying estate as far away as Honley, then a day's travel away. He does seem to have been a very competent man, much trusted by Ann Walker, Anne Lister, George Mackay Sutherland and his son as he dealt with their financial affairs, often involving large sums of money.

By 1851 Ann Walker was back at another Crow Nest estate house, Cliffe Hill, with a housekeeper, Lydia Fenton, as by then the last of her spinster aunts, ninety-year-old aunt Ann Walker, had passed away. The main Crow Nest mansion was occupied by a tenant, Titus Salt, and his family. On the 1851 census the Washingtons and their seven daughters were recorded as living at Lidgate. Even after Ann Walker died in 1854 Samuel Washington continued to act as the land agent for her nephew and heir, Evan Charles Sutherland. After Samuel Washington died in 1857 the newly married Evan Charles Sutherland Walker brought a John Smith from Scotland to be his new land agent. His and his family's connection with the churchyard is told at the end of this section.

As the Crow Nest estate was in the Lightcliffe parish many of the estate tenants and their families worshipped at St Matthew's Church and were buried in the churchyard. Renting some of the farms and other properties from the Walker family often entitled the wealthier tenants to a pew in the church as pew plaques like this one show. The first Appendix shows all of those in the West Yorkshire Archives.

James Hinscliffe (1779-1860) was a colliery owner and coal merchant who lived latterly at Knowl Top. He and many of his Hinscliffe and Cordingley relatives, as well as his wife's Hatton and Swain families, were baptised and buried in Lightcliffe. He was often in negotiations with Anne Lister of Shibden Hall for the coal on her land, and in dealings with the Rawson family over their coal interests. Anne Lister did not like James Hinscliffe's Whig politics. Her diaries record that on at least two occasions she refused to consider his son, James Hinscliffe junior (1801-1867), for positions on her Shibden Hall estate because his father was 'yellow' and not 'blue'. The first was when the lease of Stump Cross Inn came up, and then later, in 1835, he was passed over for a gamekeeper's job.

Although the Shibden Hall estate was a little further away from Lightcliffe, several the tenants and their family members were baptised, worshipped and then were buried at St Matthew's, Lightcliffe.

Sutcliffe Wood Bottom was one of the tenant farms on the Shibden Hall estate. Some of its early tenants were a Sutcliffe family, many of whose members are named on some of the earliest ledger stones in the churchyard. One member of that family, Martha Sutcliffe, married Samuel Sowden in 1799. Eventually, probably after his father-in-law died in 1815, Samuel Sowden took over the tenancy of Sutcliffe Wood Bottom. Samuel and Martha raised a large family of ten children all of whom were baptised at St Matthew's Church. Sometimes their father's occupation was "Worsted Manufacturer", sometimes "Farmer". Samuel Sowden was certainly recorded as being on the "Worsted Spinners' and Manufacturers' Committee" for the management of The Piece Hall in Halifax in the *Pigot & Co. 1828-9* directory. He was also a churchwarden at St Matthew's Church. At least two of his sons attended Hipperholme Grammar School. After school these youngest two sons, Sutcliffe Sowden and George Sowden, went to Magdalene College, Cambridge before being ordained. Rev Sutcliffe Sowden became the first vicar of Hebden Bridge and Rev George Sowden was curate in Stainland. Both brothers were friends with the Rev Arthur Bell Nicholls. Sutcliffe Sowden officiated at his marriage with Charlotte Bronte. Shortly afterwards, George Sutcliffe stayed with them at Haworth. When Charlotte died just a few months later Sutcliffe Sowden returned to Howarth to take her funeral service. Sutcliffe Sowden was tragically drowned after falling into the Rochdale Canal at Hebden Bridge in 1861. By the appointment of Archdeacon Charles Musgrave of Halifax George Sowden took over from his brother as vicar of Hebden Bridge.

Samuel Sowden (1779-1863) outlived his wife Martha Sowden (1778-1844). At the time of the 1861 census the widower, farmer and stone quarry owner, was still living at Sutcliffe

Wood Bottom with four of his unmarried adult children. The census form also records that he was blind. He was buried with his wife and three sons in the closed section of the churchyard.

The Howorth family lived at Pump and Ireland Farm, Southowram, just off Halifax Old Road on the Shibden Hall estate. Many generations of Howorths were buried in the churchyard. They were joiners and cabinet makers who would also make coffins when needed for the Listers and their tenants. And at least two Charles Howorths, grandfather and grandson, made barometers and thermometers.

In 1833 Anne Lister took a 'walking stick barometer' made by Charles Howorth senior (1765-1852) to London for valuation. His son, another Charles Howorth (1788-1863), and grandson, James, get many mentions in Anne Lister's diaries as they made bookcases, gates, doors, a shed roof, a rustic seat and the moss hut for her. The grandson Charles Howorth (1831-1899) was a joiner who made barometers and other philosophical instruments. He and his wife were also buried in the churchyard.

The rent Samuel Sowden and Charles Howorth senior paid for their Shibden Hall estate properties and land qualified them to vote in the 1835 election. It is interesting to read how Anne Lister 'helped' Charles Howorth to do this! Despite being a landowner Anne Lister was unable to vote in the West Riding election but she encouraged her tenants to vote for her preferred 'blue' candidate John Stuart Wortley, the brother of the Halifax MP. Her tenants William Hardcastle of Roydlands, Abraham Hemingway of Southolm, Mark Hepworth of Yew Trees, Thomas Pearson of Denmark Farm, George Robinson of Lower Brea and many others were subjected to this persuasion. In those days the ballot was not secret, and so it was known how individuals voted. This was how Anne Lister knew that James Hinscliffe had voted for the 'yellows', the Whigs. Some Shibden Hall tenants did as they were bid, others voted the other way, and some did not vote.

One of those who voted the other way was William Hardcastle (1784-1852), a bachelor farmer of Roydlands Farm, Hipperholme. For many years his unmarried niece Elizabeth Sucksmith (1808-1873) was his housekeeper. After William died in 1852 Elizabeth continued to run the farm near Whitehall Road, initially with her son James. She was buried in the same plot in Lightcliffe churchyard as her uncle and a one-year-old grandson.

Abraham Hemingway (1787-1850) was the son of John and Sarah Hemingway of Lane Ends, who had him baptised at St Matthew's Church in 1787. In 1818 he married Mary Exley of Lightcliffe. They went on to bring up a large family on Southolm Farm, one of the largest on the Shibden Hall estate at 42 acres. His rent was actually paid to Anne Lister's Aunt Anne but her niece still hoped to influence him and secure his vote for Wortley in 1835. In the end he was one of those who simply did not vote. Abraham joined many of his Hemingway and his wife's Exley relatives when he was buried in the churchyard in 1850. Mary then ran the farm with the help of six of their children before she passed away in 1866.

Mark Hepworth (1781-1860) and his wife Hannah were both from Heckmondwyke but appear to have moved to Lightcliffe by 1819, most probably to Yew Trees Farm where the family remained until at least 1861. Yew Trees is recorded as being 26 acres in 1835. And from the 1859 electoral roll, occupier Mark Hepworth was paying £50 per annum rent. This would have qualified him to vote in 1835 but he does not appear to have been franchised so perhaps the rent was less then. He died early in 1860 and his widow Hannah nearly three years later. Both were buried in the churchyard along with their son Richard.

Thomas Pearson (1798-1879) did do as Anne Lister asked in voting for John Stuart Wortley in the 1835 election. He was a tenant farmer and butcher occupying Denmark Farm in Southowram whose rent was paid to Anne Lister. He and his wife Mary Pearson, née Kellett, (1798-1878) had a large family many of whom were also buried in the churchyard. One daughter – unfortunately we do not know her name – was at Shibden Hall in September 1843 when Ann Walker was taken to York.

Memorandum of Robert Parker, Shibden Hall, 9th -11th September 1843

9th September 1843.

> Memorandum that this morning Captain Sutherland wished me to accompany him as his Solicitor to Shibden Hall. We took a fly and arrived there about half-past ten o'clock. The persons in the house were Mr. Short, Surgeon, York, Arthur Hedges, the Groom, John Jennings the Constable of Southowram, a little girl, the daughter of Thomas Pearson, and a daughter of Robert Mann.

11th September 1843

> Captain Sutherland and myself walked up to Shibden Hall after breakfast. Mrs Sutherland came in Mr. Edwards carriage about Eleven O Clock. I was occupied the whole day in taking down the depositions of Arthur Hedges, Robert Mann, George Thomas, John Jennings and Samuel Booth and returned home with Captain and Mrs. Sutherland in the carriage about 7 O Clock. RP.

> The persons left at the Hall were Jennings, Hedges and the two girls. RP.

George Robinson (1788-1850) was one of the sons in the business John Robinson & Sons, who were card makers, curriers and wire drawers of Hipperholme. In 1819 he and his wife moved into the newly renovated property Lower Brea on the Shibden Hall estate. He also rented Mytholm mill and other properties from the Listers. There are a number of references in Anne Lister's diaries to George Robinson. She was particularly interested in 1822 as to how the card-making was becoming more mechanised. In the 1835 election he was expected to vote for Anne Lister's preferred 'blue' candidate, but somehow he managed not to be around on election day!

John Smith (c.1820-1882) and Johanna Levack Smith née Manson (1832-1927) travelled a long way from their birthplaces in Scotland to live and then be buried in the village of Lightcliffe. They married in Wick, Caithness, in 1853, and their three eldest children were born in Scotland, in Farnell, Angus, and then in Edinburgh. Then John Smith was appointed land steward of the Crow Nest estate in Lightcliffe by its new owner, fellow Scot Evan Charles Sutherland Walker, the nephew of the previous owner Ann Walker. More children were born and baptised in Lightcliffe before tragedy struck at the very beginning of 1864. On three consecutive days in the New Year the three eldest children died.

A Smith descendant thinks diphtheria was the probable cause of death and a death certificate says 'diphtheritis'. The 10-, 8- and 6-year-old were buried together on the 5th January 1864. The Smiths' address when more children were baptised at St Matthew's was Lidgate, Lightcliffe up until 1869 when the family resided at Lower Crow Nest Farm on the Crow Nest estate. This was where John Smith farmed after the Crow Nest estate was sold, until his death in 1882. His obituary in the *Halifax Weekly Courier* on 16th September 1882 paid tribute to his progressive farming methods and his skill as a draughtsman. It was John Smith who had drawn up the plans for Lightcliffe National School when his employer Evan Charles Sutherland Walker had it built in the mid-1860s.

After John Smith's death widow Johanna and her surviving family, including more sons, appear to have then moved to Upper Rooks Farm, Norwood Green. Her 28-year-old son David Millar Smith (1867-1895) died there. He was buried with his father and young siblings.

Margaret Innes Manson (c.1834-1909) lived with her sister and nieces at Norwood Green. She was buried with her niece Susan Jane Smith (1873-1905) in a new Smith plot in the churchyard. Tragedy would strike Johanna again in 1920 when another son drowned himself in Royds Hall Dam, Low Moor Bradford. By then Johann Levack Smith was living with her only surviving daughter at 7 Norwood Terrace, Norwood Green. This was where the 95-year-old Scotswoman died in 1927.

Johanna Levack Smith and
her daughter Anne Millar Smith

6 Brief Lives

The Armytage family and Holme House.

The largest and grandest chest tomb, in the corner by Wakefield Road and Till Carr Lane, is dedicated to Mary Armytage (c.1775-1810) and the local Armytage family. When Mary died in 1810 her husband, George, must have been extremely wealthy as tombs like this were very expensive. He was a card maker, an essential part of the woollen textile process. In 1804 he bought Homestead from John Radcliffe for £1900. It had previously been called Belly Brig Hill Farm and was on the left going down to Bailiffe Bridge. He remodelled it in 1820 at the time of his second marriage to Ellen and renamed the house as Holme House. The spelling of the name does vary over time with Home also being used. When George Armytage (1769-1836) died, his eldest son, Samuel, inherited. His widow Ellen was left nothing except one or two cases of the best port in the house cellar. However, if she remarried even that was to stop.

Soon after that Holme House passed to George's brother Joseph Armytage who was both a card maker and a cotton spinner. He also owned Green House and land where the current parish church stands. In 1841 Joseph sold Holme House to the Ripley family for £5000. In the same year he sold Green House and some adjoining land to Ann Walker for £3150 but with a clause that allowed him to be a tenant there. Shortly after his death in 1849, his company went bankrupt. It looks very much as if the Armytages were the victims of the industrial revolution. Card making had been an integral part of the local wool trade whether home based or in small mills. Increasingly, carding was integrated into the new large mills and became a fully mechanised process.

Holme House stayed in the Ripley family long after they had moved away but, in its heyday, entertained a prime minister, Palmerston, and the gifted musician, Delius.

The Brooke family.

Willie Brooke (1862-1903) was accidentally killed on the railway at Lightcliffe Tunnel (under Wakefield Road at the junction with Knowle Top Road), on the 28th August 1903 aged 40 years. He was buried in the churchyard with his six-year-old son Norman Brooke (1889-1896). Two years later his wife Annie Brooke (c.1868-1905) joined them. The family monument is in the form of an obelisk near the first Till Carr Lane entrance.

Willie Brooke and Annie Sharp, who married in 1887, had three sons and a daughter. When the daughter was baptised at St Matthew's Church in 1901 her surviving brothers 'were received into the church at the same time'. The stone merchant's family lived at Hill Top House on St Giles Road.

At the time of Willie Brooke's death, he was running a company together with his older brothers, Aspinall and Newton Brooke. The company, which quarried and mined stone, was founded by their father, Joseph Brooke, in 1840. It specialised initially in the supply of the very hard Elland Flagstones found up to 90 feet below the surface. Over time Joseph bought more land between Wakefield Road and Hove Edge and his sons joined the business, and it became Joseph Brooke & Sons. In 1898 the company was developing its famous 'Nonslip Stone' which was used across the country for pavements. The company grew rapidly, buying companies in Scandinavia, the Channel Islands and near Conwy and extended into brick production. They took over the Walterclough Colliery, both for coal and clay, and constructed a large private railway running through the area and connecting to the main line at Lightcliffe Station. The large brick buildings on the left of the Brighouse Road were used mainly for chemicals during peacetime and munition production during wartime. Decline set in after the second world war and the company closed in 1969.

The founder Joseph Brooke married Grace Aspinall in 1842. Both were from Elland. They had four daughters, Hannah, Mary, Sarah and Frances, and three sons, Aspinall, Newton and William aka Willie. Fenny House, Hipperholme, at the bottom of Kirk Lane eventually became the Brooke family home. This was the home of Aspinall Brooke and his wife Rebecca Crossley, née Hunter. They married late in life in 1898 and had no children of their own but they did take in their nephews and niece, Willie and Annie's orphaned children. Aspinall Brooke (1848-1922) was buried with his parents and a baby sister at the Heywood Chapel, Northowram.

The other son, Newton Brooke, married Edith Sutcliffe in 1897. They baptised four children at St Matthew's Church when their address was Fernside, which is off Knowle Top Road. It has a carved shield bearing the initials NB on the front. By 1926, when their only daughter got married at St Matthew's Church, the family's address was The Grange on Wakefield Road (also known as New House and sometimes The Manor). When Newton Brooke (1856-1935) died he too was buried with his parents in Northowram.

His widow and bachelor sons continued to live together at The Grange until their deaths. The only son who married also moved back there from Skipton, perhaps into a separate part of the house known as Newton House which was given as his address on his probate record. Mother Edith Brooke (1872-1955) and her sons John Newton Brooke (1900-1972), Willie Aspinall Newton Brooke (1905-1982) and Edward Newton Brooke (1903-1980) and then his wife Margaret Brooke (1907-1996) were buried together in the new burial ground. Next to their impressive headstone is an almost identical but smaller one with, as yet, no inscription on it.

Alderman Mark Dawson (1819-1884)

Mark Dawson was a typical self-made West Riding of Yorkshire textile merchant, yet he was born in Manchester and also died on the other side of the Pennines. At the time of the 1841 census, he was still living with his widowed mother in Chorlton upon Medlock, Manchester. Sarah Dawson was recorded as being a shopkeeper and her son as a Cl(erk). When he married Derbyshire-born Elizabeth Mosley in 1844 his profession was given as a bookkeeper.

The Dawson family, including a son, George Frederick, and daughter, Emily, had moved from Manchester to Horton, Bradford, by 1848. They were living there in 1851 with another son, William Arthur. Father Mark Dawson's occupation was given as a worsted spinner.

Using the birth places of three more sons it would appear that the expanding family moved to Hipperholme at some time between the 1852 birth of son Mark in Bradford and the Hipperholme births of Leonard and Charles Mosley Dawson in 1856 and 1858. On all three baptism records father Mark Dawson was an agent.

By 1861 the large Dawson family was living in Lane Ends, Hipperholme-cum-Brighouse. During his time in Hipperholme he was a churchwarden at St Matthew's Church for "many" years and Trustee and President Governor of Hipperholme Grammar School. As previously noted he donated the 6th bell, duly inscribed, to the new church.

He was founder of Mark Dawson & Sons Limited of Bradford, a worsted mill. The company's name is still visible above a door, part of Springhead Mill which still exists just off Manchester Road. Mark Dawson would have known other local textile manufacturers including Titus Salt, the Ripleys and the Fosters.

In 1863 Mark Dawson was elected a Councillor for the West Ward in Bradford and was re-elected three times. He became an Alderman of the Borough in 1868. All of this suggests that he was well established, and his business was thriving. The following year he became Mayor of Bradford. His election, against fellow Alderman J Leeming, had a degree of controversy to it as the result was very close. Alderman Dawson won by "a single vote, his own."! His first year in office, however, was sufficiently successful to allow for his re-election the following year.

During the two years of his mayoralty Lister Park was bought, the ancient "soke rights" were bought out (ancient feudal rights), the foundation stones for both the Town Hall and Mechanics Institute were laid, gas works were acquired, the first School Board elected, the Free Libraries Act adopted and steps taken for the construction of sewerage works. He continued to give service to the Borough until he moved to Cheshire sometime between the mid-1870s and 1881.

By 1871 the Dawson family were living in the substantial Woodside House in Hipperholme (on Wood Lane and overlooking the A58). William Alfred was studying at Cambridge, son Mark was described as a cotton warp agent and Leonard and Charles were scholars. His wife, Elizabeth Dawson, née Mosley (c.1818-1875), died in October 1875 and was buried in Lightcliffe churchyard. A few years later in 1880 in the Strand registration district of London Mark Dawson married Elizabeth Mills from Huddersfield.

In 1881, Mark and his second wife, Elizabeth, were living in a house called Oldfield with five servants in the village of Dunham Massey, Cheshire in 1881. 62-year-old Mark was a worsted spinner and Elizabeth was 46. Mark's youngest son, 23-year-old son, Charles, a cotton spinner agent, was living with them. Eldest son George, another worsted spinner with 300 employees, was visiting. By then he and his other brothers were probably running the family business back in Bradford.

Just a few years later, in February 1884, 65-year-old Mark Dawson died. His residence, at death, was Harefield, Bowden, Cheshire. This adjoins the village of Dunham Massey next to the National Trust property. He was brought back to Lightcliffe for burial with his first wife. His funeral at the new St Matthew's Parish Church was a grand affair. The coffin and family mourners travelled by train from Bowden to Lightcliffe Station and official mourners, including the Mayor of Bradford, the Town Clerk and local dignitaries, came by a specially chartered train from Bradford Exchange. The procession from the station was led by the Chief Constable, a superintendent and 20 constables. The funeral party was met by the vicar, Rev V.R. Leonard and the choir. The organist was the already mentioned headteacher of the National School on Wakefield Road, Mr William Cook.

Mark Dawson's obituary in the *Bradford Daily Telegraph* outlines his life praising his work in the town and includes these telling words:

> *… gaining in his public life no small degree of popularity for the activity and energy with which he discharged his public duties.*

> *Somewhat brusque and impetuous in manner, he was apt to convey a less favourable impression at first sight than was created on a more extended knowledge but his energy and business tact and ability unquestioned, and the service rendered to the borough and Conservative Party were very great.*

When his second wife, the second Elizabeth Dawson, née Mills (c.1835-1892), died at Bournemouth in 1892 she too was brought back to Lightcliffe for burial in the same Dawson plot. Their memorial inscriptions note that Mark Dawson JP was 'of Dunham Massey' as well as listing some of the positions he had held.

The Hansons: cow doctors to qualified veterinary surgeons

Father William Hanson (c.1786-1868) and son Abraham Hanson (c.1808-1862) of Norwood Green were both recorded in the 1841 census as 'Farmer and Cow Doctor'. In 1845 William was paid 9s 6d for attending cattle at Cliff Hill. Other Hanson sons, either living in the same household or just next door, included two blacksmiths and a butcher. Whilst still being farmers, in 1851 the cow doctors had become horse farriers, with the other sons still following their blacksmith and butcher trades, although one son, Wigglesworth Hanson (1821-1889), had swapped his blacksmith's anvil for the butcher's knife.

It is in 1860 on a marriage certificate for Jesse Hanson (1838-1883), the son of Abraham, that the occupation 'Veterinary Surgeon' appears for the first time for both Jesse and his father. Were they qualified vets or did the knowledge accumulated in the various family businesses mean that they were called upon to treat animals by the local community? Veterinary surgeon was also how this father and son described themselves on the 1861 census. Again, at this time, the other Hanson brothers and their aged father were farming in Norwood Green as well as running blacksmith and butchers' businesses. Many of them were in the same place doing the same jobs in 1871 and 1881.

It is on the 1881 census that Throstle Nest is named as the Norwood Green residence of veterinary surgeon Jesse Hanson and his family. The Hansons continued to occupy Throstle Nest, Norwood Green, until at least 1949. In 1881 Jesse's son Abraham Edward Hanson (1862-1907) was a student at an Edinburgh veterinary college. Another younger son Arthur Hanson (1867-1905) would go on to be a veterinary assistant (presumably for his brother) in 1891 and 1901. Three generations on from great grandfather William, a cow doctor, Abraham Edward Hanson was a qualified veterinary surgeon. The initials M.R.C.V.S. appear after his name on his memorial inscription.

The Holland family

Close to Wakefield Road three William Hollands — first born sons were usually named William — are remembered on three ledger stones but the memorial inscriptions are not easy to read as a table-style tomb appears to have collapsed resulting in two of the stones being almost on top of one another. The inscriptions reveal that this Holland family originally lived at Broad Oak, Hove Edge, where some descendants still resided over one hundred and fifty years later.

The first William Holland (c.1680-1730) and his wife Grace, née Goodall (c.1681-1731) and then his son William (1712-1788) and daughter in law Hannah, née Brooke (c.1715-1789) were the earliest burials. They were followed by another William Holland (1739-1803) who was a stuff manufacturer and had a room in the Piece Hall. He, with his wife Elizabeth, née Rhodes (1740-1810) moved to Slead Hall as a tenant.

Their eldest son, a John not a William, built Slead House and Slead Syke Mill, which was situated in the Walterclough valley below where Kershaw's Garden Centre is today. This John Holland was reputed to be 'styled the Crossley or the (Titus) Salt of his day'. He and his wife, Elizabeth Hodgson, were nonconformists who had strong connections with the Bridge End Chapel in Brighouse and the Bell Metal Chapel on Bramley Lane. This Wesleyan Chapel, with a very small graveyard behind it, is now four back-to-back houses opposite Hipperholme Grammar School. When the Holland sons left the family home, Slead House, they resided at various times at New House in Lightcliffe, The Square in Halifax and at Wyke Hall. Like their father, all of them were involved in the textile manufacturing industry. Unlike their father who was buried in Halifax three of them were buried in the churchyard: William Holland (1806-1885), Samuel Holland (1809-1849) and Joseph Holland (1815-1887).

Another branch of this Holland family farmed at Hill Top and then resided in a Smith House property. This was probably not at the main house but a farmhouse or cottage from where Hollands and related Dearnleys, whose fathers were farmers, gardeners and butchers, would baptise and bury children at Lightcliffe church. Two ledger stones near the Till Carr Lane entrance have memorial inscriptions to Hollands and Dearnleys 'of Smith House'. The branch of the Holland family still farming at Broad Oak also baptised and buried family members at Lightcliffe as did their Tattersall relatives of Nab End.

John and Elizabeth Holmes and the Radcliffes of Smith House

Both John Holmes (1708-1742) and his wife Elizabeth were buried under the church. In John's case, in 1742, it would have been the original Eastfield Chapel whereas St Matthew's Church would have just been completed by the time Elizabeth died in 1785. They must have been influential people and patrons of the church to have had the honour of being buried within the church itself. The burials were recorded in the register and a simple brass plaque commemorating them is now stored in the vestry of the new church.

They lived in Smith House which was bought by John's father in 1699 and which John inherited in 1728. The family were open to nonconformist views although they remained Anglicans. John had been to London and was encouraged to meet a group of Puritans, the Moravians. He was sufficiently impressed by their faith and method of worship that he invited them to form a congregation in Yorkshire. Based initially at Smith House, John built a three-storey house known as German House alongside the coach house to act as accommodation, a place of worship and a school.

After the death of her husband, Elizabeth became more involved in early Methodism and the Moravians moved away. Those based at Smith House initially moved to Wakefield Road in Hipperholme (also known as German House, on the corner with Victoria Road) before moving away to Lower Wyke, Fulneck, Gomersall, and Mirfield. The Wyke settlement's chapel was built in 1753 and replaced in the same year as St Matthew's. It seems likely that the separation was amicable as Count Nicholas von Zinzendorf, a principal supporter of the Moravian movement, visited Smith House in March 1743.

In 1736, on their way to the American colonies, John and Charles Wesley first met some Moravians who influenced the brothers in their views and interpretation of their Christian beliefs. John Wesley was welcomed by Elizabeth Holmes to Smith House on four occasions. The first visit was on 2nd June 1742 during his first trip to Yorkshire when he preached on the theme 'Ask & ye shall receive'. His diary entry for 19th April 1774 records: 'Mrs Holmes, who has been some years confined to bed, sent and desired I would preach at her house. As I stood in the passage, both she could hear and all that stood in the adjoining house.' There was another visit on 19th April 1776 and on one other occasion when he preached from the top of the horse steps in the courtyard. Elizabeth also invited Rev Henry Venn (1725-1797), who was an Anglican clergyman who became a central figure in the English evangelical revival movement of the late eighteenth century. Elizabeth also welcomed a charismatic local preacher, Rev William Grimshaw, who had quite fundamental views.

When William Walker wanted to build St Matthew's Church, Elizabeth Holmes gave £40. In her will she also made provision for her former servant, Betty Parker, of a legacy of £40 and various items of furniture and clothing, a significant bequest. She also bequeathed £50 through a trustee to Lord North's government to support its attempt to suppress the rebellion in North America or in any other part of King George's dominions or in the defence of the realm.

After Elizabeth Holmes (1712-1785) died Smith House passed to her cousin. The large chest tomb to the left of the main entrance to the churchyard belongs to that family. Three members of the immediate family suffered mental illness and spent time in lunatic asylums, including William Towne Radcliffe who remained as a tenant in Smith House after it had passed through Charles Horncastle to Ann Walker. Ann bought Smith House and the neighbouring Hoyle House (known more recently as Harrison's Farm) for £3,750 in 1842/3 as she consolidated the estate around Crow Nest and Cliffe Hill. The house failed to reach its reserve at the 1867 auction but was then sold to Charles Dawson in 1890.

The Macauleys of Slead Hall

Some of the Macauley family lived at Slead Hall, which an early ancestor, Michael Gibson, finished renovating in 1718. He was one of the benefactors of the poor of our parish. On the death of an unmarried son Slead Hall passed to his daughter Elizabeth Gibson who had married Abraham Firth. In 1773 their daughter Ann Firth married Thomas Macauley, which is how Slead Hall came into the Macauley family.

Manchester-born Thomas Macauley was a physician as were many of his descendants. There is a slight irony that some of their Lightcliffe patients were buried nearby, and their inscriptions mention their sufferings despite the best efforts of their physicians. Thomas and Ann Macauley's two offspring, their spouses, some grandchildren and some great grandchildren were buried in five adjacent plots in the churchyard.

Ann Macauley (1781-1863) married Richard Thomas Daventry Ashworth (1772-1828), a barrister, in 1801. Although he died in Manchester, he was buried in Lightcliffe. Latterly his widow lived with her daughter and family near Doncaster and then in Beaumaris, Anglesey. When she died in Wales, she was brought back to Lightcliffe to be buried with her husband.

Ann's brother Abraham Firth Macauley (1775-1823), was a surgeon. He and his wife Mary Ann Redfern (1783-1848) who he married in 1806 had a large family of sons. Physician and surgeon son Charles Harold Macauley (1809-1869) was buried in Lightcliffe as were his attorney brothers George Gibson Macauley (1808-1842) and Francis Edwin Macauley (1809-1862) but staff surgeon Arthur Frederick Macauley (1818-1855) died of dysentery in Turkey.

Brewer and farmer Thomas Firth Macauley (1807-1874) and his wife Mary Aspinall buried five infant children and then two adult children in the churchyard. They are all remembered in a transcribed memorial inscription but unfortunately the original tombstone is no longer there. Another daughter, Louisa Macauley (1850-1876), was buried with her father and then a year later her mother, Mary Macauley (1821-1877), joined them.

Slead Hall had been the residence of Charles Harold Macauley and it then passed to his only surviving daughter Laura Ann Macauley. In 1872 she married Farquhar Forbes-Robertson. They brought up five daughters and then two sons at Slead Hall which they renovated. The two sons were both involved in WWI; one was killed in action, the other won the Victoria Cross. The widow Laura Ann Forbes-Robertson eventually sold Slead Hall to Clifford Albert Robinson sometime around 1924.

The Mann family

Five adjacent early ledger stones near one of the doors of the now demolished church all have inscriptions to individuals with the surname Mann. There was also a farm or smallholding in the area known as Mann's Farm which was on the north side of Wakefield Road just before Holme House with most of the farmland on the opposite side of the road. The earliest date on one of these ledger stones is 1696 for "Thomas the son of William Mann of Lightcliffe". William Mann had married Rebecca Batley in 1692. According to the same ledger stone William and Rebecca had fourteen children, some of whom had their baptisms at Eastfield Chapel recorded once baptism records began in 1704. Most of the offspring seem to have been buried in the churchyard – people did not stray far in those days. Commemorated on the various ledger stones are infant Manns, young children and teenagers and then a number of adult Manns. At least three married daughters were either remembered on the Mann family memorial inscriptions or with their own families on Bateman and Rushworth memorials.

One of the surviving sons, another Thomas Mann – names of deceased children were often used again – went on to baptise at least eleven children from 1740 to 1759 at Lightcliffe where he was baptised in 1706. But a Thomas Mann 'of Hipperholme' also baptised children at Coley in the 1730s. It is difficult to work out who his wife was and indeed he may have been married more than once, perhaps explaining the two different baptism venues. There is an inscription for a Mary 'wife of the late Thomas Mann' who died in 1792. As Thomas Mann was probably the Thomas Mann of Lightcliffe who was buried in the churchyard in 1779 aged 73 we would seem to have the forename of his widow at least. Again, some of these Mann children died young but others reached adulthood.

The two oldest sons, James and William Mann, appear to have moved away from Lightcliffe but were returned for burial as were their wives and some of their children. James, a joiner, and Alice Mann are recorded as being from Little Horton, Bradford. Hightown, Birstall, was the recorded abode of William and Elizabeth Mann and some of their family.

At least three daughters, Rebecca, Judith and Esther Mann, married local men, namely Phineas Firth, John Watson and and the already mentioned James Washington. They all remained in the Lightcliffe area and were buried along with their extended families in the churchyard.

Luke Settle & family and Mrs Sunderland

Luke Settle was born in Southowram and became a whitesmith in Slead Syke. A whitesmith was either a metal worker who did the finishing work on iron and steel or someone who worked with light-coloured 'white' metals i.e., tinsmiths. It is difficult to tell whether Luke, and then his son Jubal, did the filing, lathing, burnishing and polishing of iron and steel or whether they were tinsmiths. Whitesmith was the given trade for Luke and then his son Jubal in all censuses 1841 to 1881. As well as being a whitesmith Luke Settle was a noted musician as a flautist, singer and composer of hymns.

In 1799 he married Martha Freeman and they had nine children, some of whom were baptised and buried at Lightcliffe. Both Martha, who died in 1837, and Luke Settle (1777-

1863) were interred in the same plot in the churchyard along with an infant son Benjamin and then the aforementioned Jubal Settle (1817-1883). Two other sons and their wives were also buried in the churchyard.

As the choirmaster at St Martin's Church in Brighouse Luke Settle recognised the singing talent of a young Susan Sykes and, together with John Denham, encouraged her before she was taught by Dan Sugden of Halifax. She was a founding member of the Huddersfield Choral Society and sang for many years with the Halifax Choral Society. In 1833 she sang at Lightcliffe Church at a benefit concert for Ann Sladdin (Sladden), the widow of Robert, a local cordwainer (shoemaker) and singer.

Susan Sykes achieved fame under her married name of Mrs Sunderland. She sang at the opening of Leeds Town Hall (1858) in the presence of Queen Victoria who subsequently invited her to sing at Buckingham Palace. She was known as 'Yorkshire's Queen of Song' and encouraged other singers in their early careers. The Mrs Sunderland Music Festival was established following a big concert which celebrated her Golden Wedding Anniversary and is still a major part of musical life in Huddersfield and beyond. As part of this festival there is a competition for choirs, the Luke Settle Shield, in memory of the singing teacher who discovered her.

Some family of John Shillito

Although John Shillito (1832-1915) was not buried in the churchyard, two of his four wives, a baby daughter and his in-laws were. This Northowram-born son of a farmer from Upper Brear eventually became a company director of the Co-operative Wholesale Society (CWS) and its chairman from 1895 until his death.

His early education was at the Bell School in Northowram and then the local Mechanics Institute. By the age of 10 he was apprenticed to a card maker and wire drawer. 'Wire drawer' was his occupation on all censuses 1851 to 1891 and when he married in 1856. His wife was Frances Sykes, the daughter of a deceased gardener from Hipperholme. The Shillitos lived at Harley Head when they baptised some children at Lightcliffe and then moved to Upper Brear. This was their address when baby Mary Jane (1863-1864) was buried at Lightcliffe next to her grandparents John Sykes (c.1783-1846) and Rachel Sykes (c.1789-1856). They are remembered on a flat ledger stone but unusually for this part of the churchyard the Shillito headstone is vertical. Mary Jane was joined by her mother Frances Shillito (1832-1875) and then her father's second wife Nancy Shillito (1841-1878). John and Nancy Sharpe only enjoyed a few months of married life, having wed in 1878. John Shillito's third marriage, in 1879, to Charlotte Jagger in London was also short-lived as he divorced her on the grounds of adultery with her brother-in-law. His final marriage, in 1882, was to Sarah Jane Atkinson who died in 1911.

In the meantime, John Shillito was taking an active part in Halifax life as a Justice of the Peace. He was also involved with the Unitarian Northgate End Chapel, the Halifax Industrial Society and the Halifax Sunday Lecture Society as well as serving on the Halifax School Board. For the 1891 census he was still describing himself as a wiredrawer but by 1901, when he was a visitor in Crewe, he was a merchant and then in 1911 a company director. This was because in 1883 he became a company director of the Co-operative Wholesale

Society and then its chairman. He presided over the Co-operative Congress held at Doncaster in 1903. He was a frequent traveller for the CWS including a buyers' trip to the USA. In 1913, when the CWS celebrated its Golden Jubilee, it issued a medal with the face of John Shillito displayed on one side.

His other interests included science and geographical research. As a member of the Royal Geographical Society, John Shillito entertained Captain Robert Scott at Balloon Street, Manchester, shortly before the explorer's ill-fated journey to the South Pole.

Latterly, widower John Shillito lived alone in Hopwood Lane, Halifax, with a housekeeper. This was where he died in 1915 leaving over £6000. He was buried in the churchyard of All Saints, Dudwell, with his fourth wife, Sarah Jane, and other members of the family.

Lumb Stocks, R.A. (1812-1892)

Lightcliffe-born Lumb Stocks had a long career making engravings based on the paintings of famous painters of the time. Amongst his works were *Uncle Toby and the Widow*, illustrating Laurence Sterne's *Tristram Shandy*, *The Dog* by Sir Edwin Landseer and *The Meeting of Wellington and Blucher after the Battle of Waterloo* by Daniel Maclise.

Lumb Stocks was born in late 1812 at Gaubert Hall and baptised at Lightcliffe Church by the Rev Robert Wilkinson in January 1813. His father, William Stocks, who had married Mary Lumb in 1800, was variously described as a collier, a miner and a coal mine owner when they baptised and buried children at Lightcliffe and Coley.

They sent their son, Lumb, to school in Horton, Bradford where he was taught drawing by the father of Royal Academy painter and etcher Charles West Cope. In 1827 he moved to London and became apprenticed to the engraver Charles Rolls. He first exhibited work at the Royal Academy in 1832, was made an associate engraver in 1853 and an Academician in 1871. In 1839 he married Ellen Fryer. Two of their sons, Walter Fryer Stocks and Arthur Stocks, became highly regarded painters in their day.

Back in Lightcliffe William and Mary moved from Gaubert Hall to Till Carr House. Gaubert Hall was just off St Giles Road before Hill Top. It was later demolished as the stone underneath it was more valuable than the house. Both William Stocks (1770-1836) and his widow Mary Stocks (c.1777-1864) were buried in the churchyard. Her son Lumb Stocks, an engraver, of Holloway Islington was named in her probate record.

This was the residence, specifically 9 Richmond Villas, where Lumb Stocks died in 1892. He was buried in Highgate Cemetery. His family placed a brass plaque on the north wall of St Matthew's Church in his memory.

Abraham Turner (1829-1903)

Abraham Turner, one of thirteen children, was born in Gardiner's Square opposite to the Hare and Hounds pub, a poor area of Hipperholme. His father, John, was a delver and then a stone dresser. After some schooling Abraham worked initially as a warehouseman. After he married, he became a stone merchant and was eventually quite wealthy. In 1867 he was the tenant of Laverock Hall, Hove Edge, when it was put up for sale in the Crow Nest auction (it did not sell and was eventually bought by Richard Kershaw in 1890). He lived at times at Bottom Hall, in Bramley Lane, and on Till Carr Lane. He took on public responsibilities from 1860 and was a member of the Hipperholme Local Board having been on the Board of Guardians with a responsibility for looking after the poor of Hipperholme-cum-Brighouse. When Hipperholme Urban District Council was formed in 1894 he became its vice-chairman. He was a founder member of the Hipperholme Conservative Association and was a churchwarden at St Matthew's Church. In its early days the UDC agreed the lighting of the streets by gas, purchased an ambulance carriage and planned the building of a town hall. This was opened in 1899 and the library established on the top floor in 1900.

Abraham Turner died aged 75 at his home, the impressive 'Rose Mount', Leeds Road, in 1903. He was buried in the churchyard with a distinctive pedestal style monument erected by his grandchildren.

The Walker family of Horse Shoe Inn, Lidgate

In 1822 James Walker of Lidgate was named as the licensee or landlord of the Horse Shoe Inn. He had married Hannah Parsable in 1803. Within a few years Hannah lost her husband James Walker (c.1782-1827) their son John Walker (c.1808-1833) and then their married daughter Susanna Hinscliffe (c.1802-1835), as three adjacent ledger stones in the churchyard confirm. In 1830 Susanna Walker had married James Hinscliffe junior, the son of the Lightcliffe coal merchant and coal mine owner James Hinscliffe. This may explain why widow Hannah Walker became involved in mining projects near the current scout hut and at Bottom Hall. The censuses of 1841 and 1851 record that Hannah Walker was a publican, and records from 1834 and 1845 state that this was at the Horse Shoe Inn. Hannah Walker (c.1772-1853) was buried with her husband and son next to her daughter and son-in-law and then his second wife.

The public house was originally built in 1741 and included a toll booth on the Wakefield Road turnpike. (If you look at where the house is you can see the line of the original turnpike which was changed to accommodate the railway in 1850.) The Horse Shoe Inn eventually became a private house and was remodelled and called The Poplars. The property was included in the 1867 Crow Nest auction but did not sell immediately.

The Watkinson family

George Watkinson (1814-1903) established the firm George Watkinson & Sons, wool and coal merchants, and became a very wealthy man. In 1871 he had Woodfield House built, a house that members of his Watkinson family would live at for the next ninety years. (The lodge is seen on the left coming into Hipperholme from Halifax on Leeds Road.) They were active members of the Lightcliffe community and very much involved with St Matthew's Church. After the 1903 death of George Watkinson Woodfield House passed to his eldest son, another George. When this George Watkinson (1843-1905) died just two years later his eldest son, yet another George, inherited Woodfield House and moved in with his family.

One of the grandsons Samuel Lord Watkinson (1874-1915), the second son of George Watkinson (1843-1905) was buried in the churchyard. His birth was registered in the Halifax district although he may have been born in Rossendale, Lancashire, where his mother was from and where he was baptised. He and his family lived at The Grange, Lightcliffe, from where he would first go to be educated at Hipperholme Grammar School and then Sedburgh School before graduating from Trinity College Oxford. In 1909 he married Anne Charteris, the daughter of a local doctor, and they continued to live at The Grange. (Dr Charteris lived at Amisfield House near to The Crescent, prior to that he was one of the first tenants of The Crescent.)

Samuel was a keen sportsman and a good golfer, both at the Halifax Club and more locally at Lightcliffe where he was a director. Members still compete for a trophy presented in his memory in 1927. He was also president of the Lightcliffe Choral Society. For many years he was vicar's warden at St Matthew's Church. He also helped his brother, George, to fund the new church in Northowram, providing £3,500 for the building of the tower and putting in a peal of bells. In gratitude for this donation, he was given the honour of opening the tower and ringing the first bell. Both brothers were very active governors at Hipperholme Grammar School.

He had been a county councillor since 1910 but latterly ill health had restricted his contributions. Samuel Lord Watkinson died on 31st March 1915 from heart failure following a bout of influenza. He was only 41 years old. His grave is marked by a stylish cross, one of the first to be seen when entering the churchyard from Till Carr Lane. He left over £220,000. It is in his memory that the Lady Chapel in Lightcliffe's St Matthew's was created. His wife Annie Watkinson (1871-1823) was buried with him. They had two surviving children, a son William Edward (Ted) Charteris Watkinson and a daughter, Violet Corrie Watkinson, who was born just days after her father's death. Ted eventually became a dairy farmer, but his other interests were motor racing and steam railway preservation.

Rev George Watkinson (1872-1961) was Samuel's elder brother. He married Lucy Walsh (the niece of the architect, J.F. Walsh) in 1902 and not long after this they moved into Woodfield House. At the time George was the curate at St John's Coley. In 1909 Northowram was made a parish in its own right. In 1913 the building of a new church, designed by Walsh, and dedicated to St Matthew was completed. It was mainly funded by the brothers George and Samuel Watkinson. J.F. Walsh was responsible for the designs of many buildings in our area including Lightcliffe's Arts and Crafts vicarage. For the next 48 years George Watkinson served as the vicar in Northowram. He was also an honorary canon of Wakefield Cathedral. For many years he was the Chairman of Governors at Hipperholme Grammar School and a founder member of Lightcliffe's Lodge of Freemasons.

The Watkinson brothers' sister, Emma Watkinson (1850-1923), never married and lived with her parents at Woodfield House until 1904. She then moved to The Longlands on Leeds Road which had been built for her to a design by J.F. Walsh. When she died, she left money for several causes in the area including the Royal Hospital, Halifax. She also left land next to her home and funds for the four almshouses (again with Walsh as the architect) for use by residents of the three local parishes, Lightcliffe, Northowram and Coley.

It really is quite remarkable that three families, the Walkers, the Fosters and the Watkinsons were responsible for the building of eight churches and several refurbishments.

From Lightcliffe to ...

Some family members who travelled from Lightcliffe were still remembered on their family's memorial inscriptions, even though they died thousands of miles away.

The United States of America was a popular destination for some.

Fred Booth and the T.F. Firth connection in Firthcliffe, N.Y

Tucked at the bottom of the headstone to Henry Booth is a remembrance for Fred Booth (1860-1934) who was interred in Woodlawn Cemetery, Cornwall, New York State. Within this American cemetery are several others who began life round here. Fred was born in Lightcliffe and emigrated to America at the age of 24. He had been working at T.F. Firth & Sons carpet factory just down the road in Bailiffe Bridge.

Firth's carpets, founded in 1822 in Heckmondwike, moved its offices and main manufacturing base in 1867 and became one of the largest carpet manufacturers in the world. Its carpets were used in homes around the world, in hotels, trains and ships including the QE2. It lost its independence in 1968 and the Bailiffe Bridge site closed in 2000.

In March 1886, the company first purchased a factory in Philadelphia and then bought the Broadhead Woollen Mills, transferred their machinery to the new location and continued the manufacture of worsted yarns, tapestry and Brussels carpet in 1888. This new location in the Town of Cornwall, Orange County, New York, USA, where the mill was located, was then called Firthcliffe after the Firth Carpet Company and most probably the company's home village, Lightcliffe. Cornwall lies on the Hudson River a few miles north of West Point Military Academy.

The company needed skilled workers and made the offer to some of its employees to pay for their passage and their families to their new factory and to provide housing and jobs. If any did not settle, they could return to their old jobs in Bailiffe Bridge.

Fred Booth travelled to America on the S.S. *Scythia* in 1884, married his English-born wife, Lydia Hurst, in 1885 and was to superintend the Philadelphia factory and then the Firthcliffe factory. They were granted American citizenship in 1889.

The company prospered, built further factory buildings, housing and, in 1903, a clubhouse for their employees. Many followed in Fred's footsteps but in 1908 the company was prosecuted for employing illegal immigrant labour. It was fined and some were deported back to England. At this stage the American company had a turnover of $1 million and employed around 600 workers. The company was the only employer in the town and was an independent company although the principal shareholders were still the Firth family. Frederick Booth is described at the time as General Manager, Secretary and Superintendent. Records show that Fred on his own or with his wife made several visits back to the Brighouse and Lightcliffe area.

During World War II, the American operation was sold in order to raise dollars for the UK war treasury. It then continued to operate, according to past employees, very much as a family and community-oriented business up to 1962, when it closed. The village of Firthcliffe now has a population of 5,000 and, despite a fire and understandable neglect, some of the buildings still survive.

Interesting to note that Fred Booth was apparently still working even though the 1925 census had him recorded as being retired. Other sources suggest that he retired from managing the company in 1915. Fred Booth was a trustee of the New York Military Academy where a library was named after him. Previously located in the Academic Building, the library was moved to the former residence of Brigadier General Milton F. Davis, third superintendent. Built in 1916, the building was renamed Booth Library in honour of him, a loyal friend of the academy and trustee from 1910-1934.

Fred Booth died in early January 1934. His obituary in the *New York Times* stated that he had been at the firm for 50 years, was a director of the Highlands and Quassaik Bank of Newburg, a life trustee of the Institute of Carpet Manufacturers of America and Warden of St John's Episcopal Church. Clearly a much-respected man. He was survived by his widow, daughters Mrs James Patrick and Miriam Booth and son Francis Booth of Boston.

Fred Booth died a very wealthy man and there seems to have been much wrangling between his family and the state as to how much he was worth, presumably for tax reasons. The wills and probate suggest an estimation of his worth as over half a million dollars. There was also an English probate record for a little bit less! His sister and brother, Rebecca and Albert, who were living at East View, overlooking the park and churchyard, were left $5,000. This may well explain why Fred Booth has a place of honour on the family headstone.

Some of the family of soldier Horace Shaw whose name is on the Roll of Honour in St Matthew's Church also took up the T.F. Firth's offer of work in the USA. His brother and two sisters were already in Firthcliffe, Orange County, New York State, USA before WWI started. And then as his army record says his mother joined them.

> SHAW, Sergt, Horace 200569 1st/4th Bn Duke of Wellington's Regt. Died of Wounds 3rd Sept., 1916. Age 24. Son of Mrs Ruth Ann Shaw, of Cornwall on Hudson, Orange Co., New York, U.S.A. Native of Bailiffe Bridge.

To Philadelphia, Pennsylvania

Spencer Wood, born in 1875, was the fifth child of William and Rhoda Wood of Lightcliffe and thus an older brother of the surviving WWI soldier Alfred Wood. A carpet factory, presumably T F Firth & Sons, just down the hill from them at Bailiffe Bridge employed most of the working members of the Wood family. Father William was an overlooker. In 1891 fifteen-year-old Spencer Wood was apprenticed to a designer. Before the next UK census, he had emigrated to the USA to work at the Firth's carpet factory in Philadelphia. When he petitioned for naturalisation in 1907 his application papers stated that he first arrived in the USA in 1897. He was certainly there for the 1900 USA Federal census although even in that short time interval he had been back and forth at least once. Whether this trip and at least three others in the early 1900s was for business or pleasure or both we will never know.

Then in 1908 Spencer Wood married Mary Ellen Wiles and they had a son William. Two years later Spencer Wood was a widower living with his married Wiles brother-in-law in Philadelphia. His son William was probably in Lightcliffe, although no record of this Atlantic crossing has been found. For the 1911 census an American-born grandson, two-year-old William Wood, was living at 3 Hesketh Place with his grandfather William Wood, two unmarried aunts and an uncle. This little chap probably never returned to the land of his birth.

His father visited his home country and presumably his son at least once more in 1912 when he travelled to Liverpool on the *RMS Lusitania* and then back to New York on the *RMS Mauretania* just weeks after the *RMS Titanic* went down. WWI then intervened. Widower Spencer Wood, a designer at a carpet mill, was still in Philadelphia for the 1920 USA census. Then, having been taken ill after gas poisoning, which the death record states was 'probably accidental', Spencer Wood of 164 Cumberland Street, Philadelphia died on 16th December 1922. In his 1929 English probate he left a small amount of money to William Wood, a plumber, presumably his son.

To Dunedin, New Zealand

Spencer Wood's brother Harry was also remembered on the same kerb edge of the Wood plot. He must have left these shores sometime between 1901 and 1906, although no emigration record has been found. In 1906 he married Isabella Sarah Raffills in New Zealand and they had at least two children. As his Lightcliffe memorial inscription records, 56-year-old Harry Wood died on 8th June 1936 in Dunedin, New Zealand. His Anderson Bay cemetery record stated that he was a grocer. His journey from Lightcliffe must be one of the longest.

Interestingly, another brother, Herman Wood, made three long trips to Australia and back according to his obituary. Was this to meet up with his brother Harry? At least two of the trips were taken in the 1930s after Herman retired as a 'spindle maker'. The bachelor was also a self-taught painter who entered art competitions and exhibited locally. As he lived close to the churchyard in Hesketh Place some of these paintings featured the old church and its surroundings.

To Ohio and Tennessee

In 1800 Hannah Sinclair, the daughter of William and Ann, was born and baptised at Lightcliffe but nearly 84 years later she 'was interred at Tallmadge, Ohio' according to the memorial inscription on a grave plot she had previously owned. The plot, next to her parents' plot, was where she had seen buried a baby son, a teenage son and two husbands. Hannah Sinclair married John Marsden in 1824. They baptised several children at St Matthew's Church, including a Sinclair Marsden in 1842. John Marsden died in 1847 and two years later Hannah married John Dennison. The Dennisons lived in Northowram with some of the Marsden children. Stone quarryman John Dennison died in 1863 and neither Hannah Dennison nor Sinclair Marsden have been found in the UK after that.

However, Sinclair Marsden, an Englishman born in 1842, became a naturalized American in Akron, Ohio in 1872. By the 1880 USA census his 78-year-old widowed English-born mother Hannah Dennison – and an 8-year-old 'granddaughter' – were living with him in Akron, Ohio. Hannah was keeping house but there is no indication as to what Sinclair's occupation was. Similarly, there are no clues as to when they left England, either together or separately or why.

USA deaths records confirm what is on the memorial inscription back in Lightcliffe: that the 83-year-old English-born widow Hannah Dennison died on 2nd May 1884 at Bowery St., Akron, Ohio. And then English-born Sinclair Marsden died on Christmas Day 1897 in Nashville, Davidson, Tennessee. But who put the memorial inscription on the headstone above the plot that Hannah Dennison of Northowram owned?

To South Africa

Percy Frederick Stancliffe was born in Burton on Trent in 1871. Quite why his parents were in Nottinghamshire is unclear. Two years previously an older brother was born in Galway, Ireland, and subsequent siblings were born in Suffolk and Sussex. No marriage record has been found for Halifax-born William Cockroft Stancliffe and Kent born Emma Aldridge, although the St Martin in the Fields baptism of a daughter in 1867 may be a clue. But to confuse matters William is named as the father of an 1851 Irish-born daughter when she married.

Perhaps father William's occupation explains the family's necessary itinerant nature. When William C. Stancliffe became a member of the Grand Lodge of Freemasons of Ireland he was a 'Supervisor of Excise'. When visiting his sister in Ovenden in 1881 he was a 'Supervisor Inland Revenue', but by 1891 the taxman had become a postmaster at Towngate Hipperholme, retiring to a house named Mayroyde on St Giles Road by 1901.

Meanwhile, two of his sons, Percy and Ernest, had become soldiers. Appropriately, Irish-born Ernest became a Lieutenant in the Royal Irish Regiment. In 1890 the architect and surveyor Percy Frederick Stancliffe signed up for 12 years with the Royal Engineers. After serving in both Central and South Africa he returned to South Africa as a policeman. The memorial inscription on his parents' Lightcliffe headstone indicates that this was where he died in January 1906.

The headstone also notes the previous deaths and Lightcliffe burials of his father William Cockroft Stancliffe (1824-1904) and a sister Edith Olive Alice Stancliffe (1867-1891). In 1908 Ernest William Temple Stancliffe (1869-1908), by then an insurance agent, joined them. Another sister, Edith Winifred Stancliffe had married Benjamin Casson in St Matthew's Church in 1899. Widow Emma Wesley Stancliffe (1839-1911) lived with the Cassons at Abbotsford, Lightcliffe, before she died.

To Antwerp

Many Sucksmiths were baptised and buried at Lightcliffe, including the WWI victims. Some had smallholdings in Norwood Green. One such family was that of John and Rachel Sucksmith who baptised at least seven children at St Matthew's, including a son William in 1815. At the time of the 1841 census William was living with his parents and siblings. His father was a farmer, but 25-year-old William was a 'Leather Currier' which may or may not explain what he was doing in Antwerp where he died in 1863, as noted on his parents' headstone:

Also of William, son of the above who died at Antwerp
November (2nd) 1863 aged 48 years.

To Naples

The earliest memorial inscription for a Lightcliffe-born individual who died on foreign soil was for John Walker junior. As already described, this young man, who inherited the vast Crow Nest estate, died on his honeymoon in Naples in 1830. He was buried at the old Protestant cemetery on Corso Garibaldi in Naples which had been bought by the British Consul in 1826. In 1980 the British Consul gave this cemetery as a park to the city of Naples, and most of the bodies, including John's, were moved to the new Poggioreale municipal cemetery. He was therefore twice buried, like several of our WWI soldiers who were also reburied after the Great War ended.

Back in Lightcliffe Fanny Walker, née Penfold, had this memorial to her husband John Walker placed on the southern wall of the old church. The memorial survives to this day and now resides in the tower.

Interestingly, one of Fanny's younger brothers, Dr Christopher Rawson Penfold (1811-1870), and his wife, Mary, emigrated to Australia. Christopher, a physician, was a believer in the medicinal benefits of wine and both he and Mary planned to concoct a wine tonic for the treatment of anaemia. Christopher had set up his practice on the eastern outskirts of Adelaide. Initially, the Penfolds produced fortified wines for Christopher's patients. As demand for the wines increased, the winery was expanded and was officially established in 1844. The Penfolds discovered that clarets and Rieslings were both easy to produce and popular. The business grew and is now part of one of the largest wine businesses in Australia.

7 Churchyard burials

Introduction

We do hope that you will want to look round our churchyard. This chapter is intended as stand-alone with a general description of burials and then gives you a tour. If you have read the book, inevitably there will be some repetition.

There are over 11,000 burials in the churchyard, most of which can be looked up on the Burial Search section of our web site www.lightcliffechurchyard.org.uk. They date from 1674 to the present day. Although parish records do not seem to begin until 1704, we have eleven burials before then. All eleven are in known grave plots and all but one have detailed memorial inscriptions. Therefore, we know either the death or burial date for these individuals and in some cases their age. These details may have been added later after the death of other family members who were then buried in the same plot.

Matthew Caygill died 11th July 1696   John Whittaker died February 1692

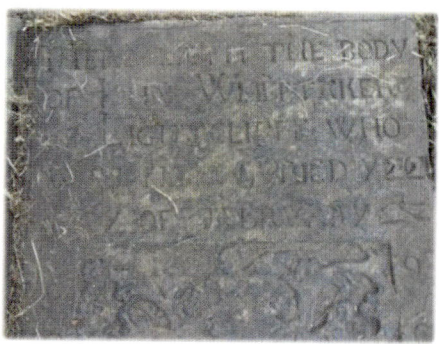

Only the year was recorded for the five burials in 1704 when three of the five had the surname Brook. Edward Brook, the husband of Grace, who died in 1704 and who was possibly the father of a child who also died in 1704, was buried on 5th November 1705 in an unknown grave.

The early graves are in the section of the churchyard that surrounded the old church next to Wakefield Road. When that was closed, following the 1853 Burial Act, burials began to take place in the middle section. A third section, which is still used today, was added later.

The very young to the very old and all ages in between.

The age range of those interred in the churchyard range from hours old to over 100 years.

The little white cross was for David Watkinson, son of Samuel Lord Watkinson, who was buried in a plot owned by his maternal grandfather Dr William Charteris of Amisfield House, Hipperholme. The parish register records that he was just 7 hours old when he died on 1st September 1911. Dr Charteris's own baby daughter had been buried in the same plot over forty years earlier in 1870 aged 8 months.

Other infants barely survived much longer and in some cases their mothers died about the same time, a solemn reminder of the perils of childbirth in those days. The two Hanson deaths in 1674 were of Esther, wife of Robert Hanson, and Judith, daughter of Robert Hanson so this may well be the first example of a mother and her baby dying not long after the birth. The previously mentioned Brook family may provide another example.

Then there were the various childhood illnesses and diseases to avoid such as chicken pox, smallpox and measles. Many infants are recorded as simply buried in an unknown grave, perhaps one that just happened to be dug for another committal. Some are named, such as William, Robert and Fanny Emily, who died in infancy, the children of John and Hannah Williamson. Others have no name; the inscription just records "and five children died in infancy." Scarlet fever, diptheria and cholera could strike at any age and often resulted in family members succumbing at about the same time. John and Johanna Smith's children died on successive days from diptheria.

However, for those who survived into adulthood, and despite the fact that average life expectancy was obviously lower than it is today, many occupants of the churchyard lived to a ripe old age. There are 22 nonagenarians in the parish registers pre-1920 and proportionally many more after then. But the oldest individual was centurion Mary Ripley of Slead Syke. She was recorded as being 100 years and 11 months old when she was buried on the 13th February 1825.

As now, accidents did happen. Sometimes this was recorded on the gravestone as this memorial to Willie Brooke (1863–1903) states. He was the youngest son in the firm Joseph Brooke & Sons.

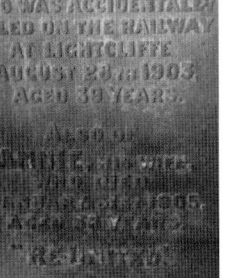

Similarly on a Rushworth plot:

In loving memory of Arthur Rushworth
the beloved son of John Lister and Sarah Ann Rushworth
of old Godley Lane Halifax who lost his life
in the North Bridge Tram disaster on July 1st 1906 aged 24 years.

Another earlier 'accident' in 1819 on North Bridge was actually a murder. The Mr Asquith 'thrown over the battlements of the North Bridge, at Halifax, and killed on the spot' may well have been Joseph Asquith of Lane Ends, Hipperholme who died on 23rd May 1819 aged 46 years.

There were a number of stone quarry mines in the Hipperholme and Lightcliffe area but they were dangerous places to work. The Broad Oak Quarry, Hipperholme was where Richard Jowett (1849–1892) and another man were killed instantly when they fell 90 feet. They and two others were being lowered in a box which tilted and got caught on the side of the shaft tipping the men out. The two other men clung to the cage and ropes and so escaped unhurt.

Falling stones were another hazard. A large stone dislodged and killed Alfred Pearson (c.1855-1895) at the Yew Tree Stone Quarry owned by father and son Collins. Just over a year later at the Kerb Royd Stone Mine the son James William Collins (1862–1896) suffered a severe head injury from which he died in Halifax Infirmary a few days later. An inquest concluded that the injury had been caused by 'a very small piece of stone, weighing two or three ounces, falling a distance of 20 yards'. In 1902 at Nab End Quarries a flat stone weighing about three tons was being raised by means of a crane, when the chain broke, and the stone fell on father Thomas Collins (1837-1903) fracturing his left thigh and injuring both legs.

Daniel Batty (1863-1903) and his wife Alice née Preston named their eldest son Preston Batty (1846-1893) for obvious reasons. In 1871 the 25-year-old wire drawer enlisted with the Scots Guards. When he was discharged in 1883 after serving for 12 years, he probably returned to Hipperholme. During the summer of 1891 he was found by a local constable sleeping rough. This resulted in him spending a month in HMP Wakefield for being a 'Rogue & Vagabond'. Two years later he was employed at the Hipperholme brewery of Messrs Brear & Brown. One summer's evening in 1893 he attempted to climb the 'Jacob's Ladder' into the hay loft of his employers' stable. He fell and fractured the base of his skull. He was taken to Halifax Infirmary but never regained consciousness and died within hours.

Some drownings were probably suicides.

William Nicholl (c.1823-1869), an employee in the grounds of Sir Titus Salt's Crow Nest estate, was found drowned in the Crow Nest Lake which was only three foot six inches deep. The inquest into the death of Harry Senior (1847–1899) reported that he was 'Found drowned without a mark of violence, having probably drowned himself, but there is not sufficient evidence to show the state of his mind at the time.'

However, most people died of natural causes.

The first burial in many grave plots was often that of a young child. That prompted a family member, usually the father, to buy a plot, sometimes adjacent plots, where other family members were then interred. The grave owners were often recorded in the burial records and sometimes on the memorials themselves. Then you can follow the grave being subsequently owned by a widow, children and even grandchildren. A number of individuals were brought back to Lightcliffe to be buried in the family plot even though they died elsewhere.

Almost all graves are orientated west-east from an early belief that at the final judgment call the body would rise and face Jerusalem.

Memorials

Lightcliffe is typical of many rural Anglican churchyards in this area. There are few imposing memorials such as those that you will find in Coley churchyard, Lister Lane cemetery or Undercliffe in Bradford. Many are simply carved in local sandstone. This is a great boon as it proves resistant to erosion and what was written 300 years ago is still clear today. Even the chest tombs which must have been expensive are fairly simple with little ornamentation.

Most of the memorials in the oldest section of the churchyard are flat stones. These ledger stones were designed to cover the grave. They were never erected vertically and laid flat later. The coffin of the first occupant would be buried well below the surface. As others of the family died, the ledger stone would have been moved to one side, the earth removed, the new coffin buried, and the stone replaced. Between these stones there are patches of grass. These were unmarked graves, in some cases another family grave, and in others used as needed. Parishes had a coffin for common use which was emptied of the body at the time of burial and then reused – an early example of recycling.

Quite recently the ground below the turf has been archaeologically surveyed. There are no ledger stones hidden beneath the grass.

As well as a handful of chest tombs there are a few examples of table tombs (these are subject to collapse, see the Hollands' family plot near Wakefield Road) and a few cope tombs. In all these cases, the bodies were buried as normal, underground.

A chest tomb

A table tomb

A cope tomb

From the early Victorian era onwards a more recognisable headstone became the style, sometimes with a kerb surround to the grave and, occasionally, with a footstone. The first use of a cross as part of the headstone is in 1860, this may be because a stricter Protestant view of iconography prevailed. By the middle of the century there were movements encouraging the greater use of imagery in the Anglican church.

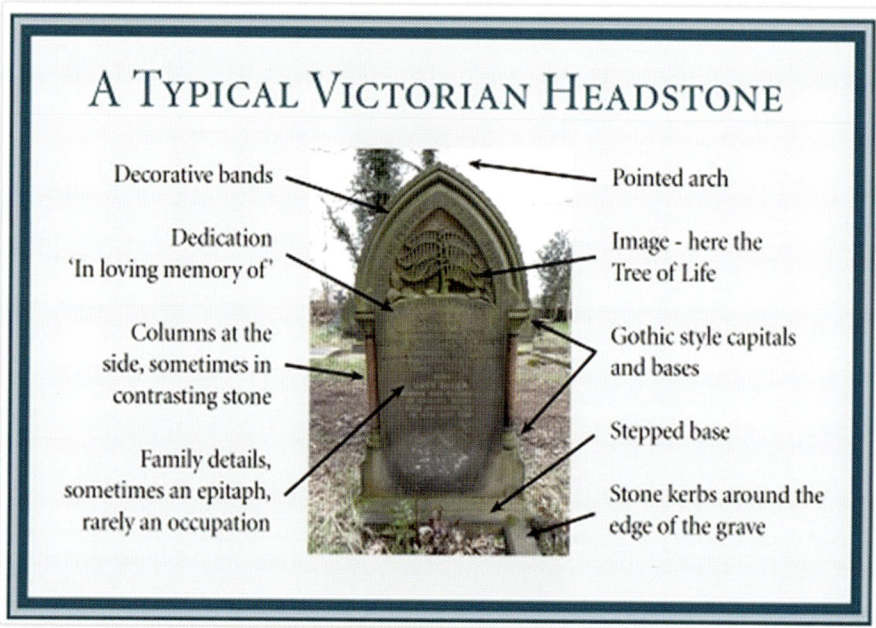

A TYPICAL VICTORIAN HEADSTONE

Decorative bands

Dedication
'In loving memory of'

Columns at the
side, sometimes in
contrasting stone

Family details,
sometimes an epitaph,
rarely an occupation

Pointed arch

Image - here the
Tree of Life

Gothic style capitals
and bases

Stepped base

Stone kerbs around the
edge of the grave

From this period a greater variety of grave memorials began to appear including an obelisk, crosses on a pile of stones representing Golgotha and variations on the typical Victorian headstone.

Other graves included kerbstones with or without a raised headstone (banned almost everywhere nowadays because of the difficulty of mowing round them) and pedestal memorials which come in many variations. There is evidence that several of the graves had been surrounded by iron railings as was the churchyard itself. They were probably removed in 1940 as part of the war effort.

Non-local material such as granite and marble began to appear – but never in quantity – in the middle of the 1800s as transport costs dropped when the railways came to the area. Our earliest examples are from 1859.

From the earliest days there are examples of images on the memorials. They had specific symbolism initially but, possibly, later some were used primarily as decoration.

- Angels: represent resurrection, the soul on the way to heaven or praying. We have traditional versions and an Art Deco style.
- Bones: thigh and scull: mortality.
- Heart: love, charity.
- Books: the Bible, resurrection through scripture, knowledge and, on at least two, the open book forms part of the grave itself.
- Trefoil: Holy Trinity.
- Trumpet: victory over death and resurrection
- Crown: immortal crown of Christian life.
- Hands: friendship or brotherly love: there are clasped hands barely visible on one of the oldest ledger stones.
- Draped urn: head of household.
- Trees and plants: life – also broken tree or cut flower meaning death

The symbol that might be most expected, the cross, is not found here until the mid-C19 – as with other images there was a possible association with Catholicism.

Memorial Inscriptions

The memorial inscriptions are of great help to those tracing their family history. They provided the opportunity to give details of those buried e.g. names, dates, ages, abodes, relationships. It is particularly helpful when individuals who died elsewhere were noted on the family headstone.

The stone would have been quarried in the area, prepared and often beautifully carved by local craftsmen who were unlikely to have been specialists. This probably explains the non-standard approach to the spelling of names and the setting out of the text. Arriving at the end of a line, some words were simply wrapped round on to the next line. Alternatively, abbreviations as superscripts were sometimes squeezed in. A good number of the carvings were supplemented with lead and a few still have evidence of red and black paint. There were probably more done in this style but over time they will have faded and disappeared. Similarly, on the very few headstones where local stone was not used, erosion has made their inscriptions very difficult to read.

Epitaphs

There are very few epitaphs where the inscription relates directly to the person buried. There is a reference to 'a loving & indulgent father' which, perhaps, is unexpected in mid-Victorian times. Other examples include:

> *Reader, here lies entombed a virtuous wife whose sweet deportment graced this mortal life, secured her husband's love and friends applause till death removed her from this vale of woe. (1783)*

> *She that doth here rest within this tomb had Rachel's face and Leah's fruitful womb, Abigail's wisdom, Lydia's faithful heart, Martha's care but Mary's better part.*
> *Farewell my wife and children dear, I've toiled with you from many a year. I always strove to do my best and now I'm gone to take my rest. (1884)*

We are still looking for Elizabeth Mallinson, 1789, a true paragon of virtue.

> *In mental abilities exceeded by few, in industry by none, no wonder then that she did most good and that many lamented her loss. Faults she had some and several frailties, or she would have been more than woman. But sloth, envy, malice hold thy hand nor dare to rake for them amongst her sacred ashes in this awful hallowed place, but let them rest with her in the dust unmentioned and unmolested till that tremendous day when she must give an account to her impartial Judge to whom alone she is accountable and when her good action rush upon thy memory; go thou and do likewise.*

Two inscriptions may give a reason that there are not many epitaphs praising the dead:

> *No verse of praise write on my tomb.*
> *There is a judgment yet to come.*
> *Leave all to God who justly knows*
> *and more than we deserve*

There are also a few quotations from the Bible:

> *Thou wilt keep him in the perfect peace whose mind is stayed on thee because he trusteth in thee.* Isaiah Chap 26 ver 3.

> *The grass withereth, the flower fadeth but the word of our Lord shall stand for ever.* Isaiah Chap 10 ver 8.

> *Blessed are the peacekeepers for they shall be called the children of God.* Matthew Chap 5 ver 9.

There are also quotations from the services such as,

grant her eternal rest and let light perpetual shine upon her.

However, there are many indicating a strong belief in heaven and a reuniting at the last judgment, for example,

Blessed are the dead which die in the Lord.

What is clear is that there were books of possible inscriptions available to families to choose an appropriate one. Some are repeated not just here but in other churchyards across the country.

If we need reminders that ill health was a major concern for all ages and for rich and poor then these are examples:

long in this life I've been in pain

After life's fitful fever, rest.

Oh cruel death that would not be denied
that broke the knot that was so recently tied.
                         (Reads as though death came early in married life, 1842)

Slowly her earthly frame decayed, her end was long in sight.
Nor was her steady soul afraid to take its awful flight.
A pale consumption gave the fatal blow.
The stroke was certain but the effect was slow. (1785)

Long in this world I've been in pain
and all physicians were in vain
till Christ in mercy gave me rest
and called me hence where I am blest.

There are several contrasts between the long and painful period of death of some and the sudden and unexpected deaths of others.

Certainly, for children, 'suffer little children to come unto Me' is a common inscription as are these:

Short was our earthly life ...

Ah, not in cruelty, not in wrath, the reaper came that day,
'twas an angel visited this green earth and took the flower away.

Within this silent tomb lies slumbering here,
the dust of these three children dear,
free from all pains pride malice and sedition,
happy they that be in this condition. (1778)

'Ere sin could blight or sorrow fade,
death came with friendly care,
the opening bud to heaven conveyed
and bade it blossom there. Aged three weeks (1798)

There seems a shadow on the day
his smile no longer cheers.
An angel visited the green earth
and took the flower away. 14 months old.

There are also warnings to be had:

Behold my friend and cast an eye
Then go thy way, prepare to die
Repent with speed, make no delay.
I, in my prime, was called away. (1851) (He was 73 – some prime!)

Take ye heed, watch and pray for you know not when the time is. (1914)

With solemn aire, spectator view my fate.
You thus must pass to an immortal state,
seriously think on your eternal home,
a dying saviour and the life to come.
Now while time is given to Mercy fly
nor wait tomorrow lest tonight you die. (1794)

I little thought when I left home,
my race was so near run.
But ah alas death called me home.
I never did return.

Stand reader here and spend a tear
and think on me who now lies here.
And whilst thou readst the fate of me
think on the glass that runs for thee.
Let not this world thy thoughts betray
but think upon thy dying day.
… prepare thyself to follow me.

Though we have some mention of occupations, there is only one inscription of any detail – and this can be found elsewhere in other churchyards:

My anvil and hammer lie declined,
my bellows too have lost their wind.
My fire's extinguished and my forge decayed
and in the dust my vice is laid.
My coals are spent, my iron's gone.
Last nail I drove, my work is done.

One inscription reminds us that, in death, all are equal:

Stay Reader meditate a while on Death
Think though ere long must yield thy fleeting breath
The old, the young, the monarch and the slave
are all by nature destined to the grave.

A sad inscription for Joanna died in 1883 aged just 20:

She longed to go home, she was weary here,
She wrestled with sin for many a year,
And if she had stayed she must still wrestle on,
For the flesh would not rest till the spirit had gone.

The inscription on the grave of John Hatton in 1792 sums up both suffering and belief in the future life:

who after a painful affliction which he bore with the patience and resignation of a true Christian under a firm confidence through Christ of a glorious resurrection departs this life universally respected

Names, where they lived and what they did.

It is interesting to look at the names on the headstones. In the first 150 years, almost all female names were biblical, such as Mary, Sarah, Martha and Elizabeth. Similarly, for men the Old Testament names such as Joseph and Joshua are common, and Abraham was more popular than it is now. Henry, John, Richard, Robert, Thomas and William appear quite frequently from the earliest period whereas the first examples of George, Charles and Anthony are not seen until the late C18 and early C19.

At the other end of the scale these Old Testament names were extremely rare; Abednego (servant of Nego), Absolom (son of David), Achsah (aka Accy! daughter of Caleb), Banzillai or Barzillai (the Gileadite), Amaus, Cain, Caleb, Elkanah (husband of Hannah, father of Samuel who was a polygamist), Emmanuel, Ephraim (son of Joseph), Gabriel (the archangel), Hezekiah, Israel, Japhet (son of Noah), Keziah (a daughter of Job), Manaseeh, Naomi, Salome (meaning 'peace'), Thirza, Tamar (meaning 'date palm tree'), Zaccheus and Zillah (wife of Lamech). The last Old Testament name, Uriah, died in 1934.

Amongst other first names occurring just once are Alvina, Ambrosine, Beaumont, Bradley, Charity, Cicely, Cordelia, Damaris, Emmett, Esquire, Ffaris, Ffarth, Gervase, Hamilton, Harper, Humphrey, Jervice, Laneforth, Lawton, Lockwood, Luther, Mario, Marmaduke, Mason, Middleton, Myra, Needley, Osbert, Osbourne, Palisme, Pamelia, Philemon, Prudence, Rahenu, Randolph, Septimus, Sylvanus, Tabitha, Tempest, Valentine, Valinda and Verona.

The surnames come as no surprise. Many names were and remain local: Hemingway, Mallinson, Marsden, Smith, Sharp(e), Robinson, Robertshaw, Naylor and so on. Some of these surnames and others were also used as first names. There was quite a long period when it was common to take the mother's or grandmother's maiden name as a first name

There are a number of examples where the first-born has this maiden name for example, Sucksmith Broadley, Mallinson Hall and Bottomley Kershaw as well as the already mentioned Aspinall Brooke, Preston Batty, Sinclair Marsden and Lumb Stocks Then there are other examples where the family seem to have resorted to using surnames such as Dyson, Fox, Hartley, Jagger, Newton, Wilson and others, perhaps having run out of 'ordinary' first names. And sometimes it became a family tradition. Midgeley Marsden was baptised in 1819 with his mother's maiden name after Betty Midgeley married Abraham Marsden in 1809. Then when he married Ann Schofield in 1841, they named a son Schofield Marsden. But Schofield Marsden and his wife Edna Smith did not use the first name Smith. There are, however, two individuals, Smith Tattersall and Smith Womersley, and a number of others with Smith as their middle name, buried in the churchyard. Perhaps the 'best' example of the use of a maiden name was for a son of William Shooter and his wife Naomi, née Sharp. Little Sharp Shooter was possibly named without his parents thinking of the alternative meaning. A sharpshooter was a term in common use for 50 years before this little chap was baptised at St Matthew's Church in 1867.

It is also clear that within the small local population many of the families were closely related. Where they lived in the neighbourhood is also of interest. As you would expect, the majority are from the immediate Hipperholme and Lightcliffe area. From 1714 we begin to see that people from slightly further afield, such as Wy(i)ke, might be buried here. William Long was from Preston Parish. Belly Bridge (for Bailiffe Bridge) is mentioned in 1744 for the first time and continues to appear along with Bailiffe Bridge itself until 1828. Lower Brookfoot, Upper Green, Hove Edge, (also Hussedge), Lower Bonegate, Priestley Green, Norwood Green, Birstall, Hartshead, Helliwell Syke, Hargreaves Head, Slead Syke, Shelf, Hightown, Cleckheaton, Sutcliffe Wood Bottom, various parts of Southowram including Pump, and Thornhills are all recorded. The actual address was rarely recorded on a headstone as it was in parts of Wales. There it identifies which Jones or Williams it is!

Some specific homes – Lidgate, Coley Mill, Brookfoot Mill (Southowram), Smith House, Yew Trees, Slead Hall, High Sunderland, Rooks, Dumb Mill, Soup or Soaper Hall, Hoyle House, Crow Nest, Southedge House, Stafford House, German House, Gawbert Hall (just off St Giles Road, later to become a quarry site), Lower Winteredge, Sauf (Sough) Hall, Cliff Hill, Little Ireland (possibly the farm on Halifax Old Road), Denmark Farm, Mytholm Farm, Laverock Hall, Dove House, Sawood House, Lough Hall and so on – do get a mention. Bottom Hall appears in the Burial Registers as does 'Workhouse', which could be the same place as the workhouse was based there at the time of these entries. Several entries from here are for relatively old individuals aged over 70 as we are dealing with a time without pensions.

There is a significant number of individuals from parts of Southowram. Apparently, it was relatively expensive to be buried in the churchyard there perhaps because the bedrock was close to the surface and would take some digging out.

Some who died out of the area were brought back to Lightcliffe for burial, for example Mark Dawson from Dunham Massey and Charles Robinson from Altrincham. Others who had to be buried elsewhere are remembered on family headstones. Overseas countries that feature in memorial inscriptions include Belgium, France, Ireland, New Zealand, South Africa, Turkey and the USA.

There are very few indications of occupations. For many it was not important in death; for others, everyone would have known them as the local landowners or the village blacksmith, publican, wheelwright or whatever. Some occupations can be inferred, such as priests with a title Reverend. The first, recorded in 1724, was Abraham Hanson, a cleric. There are nine priests in all including three incumbents of St Matthew's, and Matthew Stanley, a Congregational minister. Some were career soldiers such as Dragoon Joseph Naylor (Crimean War) and Sergeant Major Fred Mitchell (died German South West Africa, 1915); others were volunteers and conscripts in WWI.

According to his memorial inscription Benjamin Beaumont, who died in 1742, was a 'butcher, husband and father'. The burial record when John Overend, son of Joseph, died in 1749 notes that he was a wiredrawer, as was Joseph Green of Watergate. One hundred years later members of the family firm John Robinson & Sons, many of whom were buried in the churchyard, were also wire drawers as well as card makers and curriers. John Medley of Priestly Green, who also died in 1749, was the Clerk of Coley. One individual, Laneforth Dawes, was recorded as a vagrant and another as a pauper. On William Mallinson's headstone it is recorded that he was a "Mason who erected this Chapel". The initials M.R.C.V.S. are carved below a Hanson cross. Members of this Hanson family started out as cow doctors and then some of them became trained veterinary surgeons. The C.E. after George Duncan's name stands for Civil Engineer.

The nineteenth-century census records allow the occupations of many individuals to be looked up even if there is no clue in either the burial records or on the headstone. The 1841 census records many as simply M.S. or F.S. standing for Male Servant or Female Servant. The large houses had an army of servants – butlers, valets, maids, cooks, laundry maids, scullery maids, gardeners, grooms and later chauffeurs – but even more modest households often had servants. Many were local folk who would never move out of the neighbourhood. One exception was a Clifton-born girl who was a servant for the Listers at Shibden Hall. As lady's maid to Anne Lister, Elizabeth Wilks Cordingley travelled with her mistress on many excursions around Yorkshire, further afield and even to Paris. She left the Lister's employment early in 1835 and a year later married William Parkinson, a farmer from Lower Rookes. Elizabeth Wilks Parkinson (1788-1864) of Laverock Lane was buried in an unknown plot within the closed churchyard on 29th March 1864, but she had seen more of the world than most of her contemporaries.

Amongst the eleven thousand individuals buried in the churchyard there are architects, bookkeepers, coopers, dress makers, engine drivers, farmers, governesses, headteachers, innkeepers, joiners, kerb stone manufacturers, land agents, merchants, nurses, overseers, printers, quarry owners, railway labourers, saddlers, tanners, undertakers, vergers and worsted spinners but no x-ray machine operators, yachtsmen or zookeepers!!

8 The TOUR starts here

To the left of the main entrance is one of the largest and oldest chest tombs, belonging to Charles and Charlotte Radcliffe. A sad story in that Charlotte died quite young and her two children were both declared, in the terms of the day, lunatics. William Towne Radcliffe died at the age of 78 in Smith House. His sister, Charlotte Lucretia Francina died in York possibly in an asylum. Their gardener at Smith House was James Sykes of Spring Gardens, Waring Green. He was the father of the singer Susan (Susannah) Sykes who became well known as Mrs Sunderland.

On both sides of the main path are some quite old stones but the earliest tend to be further over to the right. However, one to look for is halfway to the tower, three rows in from the path on the left. This is dedicated to William Mallinson, the mason who was responsible for building the church. Close by is the grave of Samuel Sowden, two sons of whom became successive vicars of Hebden Bridge. However, he never had a son named Thomas, who killed him and fed him to the pigs as told in the TV series *Gentleman Jack*. Samuel lived a long and successful life.

When you get to the tower look and see how the right-hand side has been rebuilt when the church building was demolished. Looking at the side with the door, you can see how it has been filled in and rendered. Part way up, there would have been the entrance from the tower to the gallery. On the furthest side, you can see where the lean-to vestry stood. While here, look at the partial outline of the old church. You can make out where the doors were and visualise the apse at the far end.

There were just a few burials under the church. Initially, these were for the clergy though this later was extended to patrons of the church such as Elizabeth Holmes or members of the Walker family. Rev Wilkinson was buried in the church in 1839. The last Walkers to be buried were Mary, Ann and their niece Ann. They were buried in vaults (the furniture would have had to be removed to gain access) and sealed with stone lids. Most would have been remembered by memorials on the walls or brass plaques. That for Ann Walker junior remains in the tower as does a marble memorial for Rev Richard Sutcliffe. Others are stored in the new church.

If you turn left and walk along the short path you will notice some old ledger stones which are well worn. One looks to have some form of armorial display, but it is by no means clear.

Walk across the grass towards the western wall passing two prominent headstones, one to William Berry and the second to Rev William Gurney.

Near the wall are several graves which have stories to tell. There is one with a warning not to mess with this grave which coincides with the time of the body snatchers. This is for Jane Woodhead in 1825.

Let no rude hand with spade prepare
To dig the dust that's buried here
But let it rest in this its bed
Until the graves give up their dead.

Close to the wall you may find the grave of Samuel Washington, the land agent for both the Walker estate and that of Shibden Hall. Then, a row or so in from the wall, are two graves commemorating the soldiers who died in the Crimean War. You might see the reference to Scutari where Florence Nightingale reformed the hospital. Further on, by the rhododendron bush, is the chest tomb of George Mackay Sutherland. It looks as though he had expected others of the family to be buried here. At his feet, is the grave of John Smith, his son's land agent. The poignant inscription tells of his dreadful losses in January 1864. You will see many examples of infant deaths; the rich were not immune to such tragedies. Other inscriptions tell of deaths associated with childbirth, a very dangerous time for both mother and child. There are several examples of a child dying to be followed within days of the mother or the other way round.

Infant mortality rates were high for much of the period covered by the churchyard. Many more died before they reached 20. However, there are also many examples of longevity. You will not need to look far to find people living until they were 80 or more.

Just before returning to the path, you will see our only 'footstones' at the base of graves dedicated to the Carter family of Giles House and then look at the ledger stones for Wilkinson and Fenton, daughters of a curate. Once reaching the path, there is a fine example of a cope-style chest for Sarah Walton, who is remembered in the new church. We are coming now to the end of the 'closed' part of the churchyard. Over to the right of the path, you would notice that there are no early ledger stones. This is because until 1800 or so, it was thought by some that the land to the north of a church belonged to the devil. What you will see is that the ledger stones near to the boundary of the old church are deeper than elsewhere. This is the result of the landscaping after the church was pulled down.

Just before coming to the cross path look for two headstones. One commemorates the deaths of the two Pybus boys, one a Grenadier and the other in the Royal Flying Corps, who died in WWI, and another, to the Booth family, remembers a successful American businessman buried in New York State, you will need to look very low down on the headstone. Not all headstones were plain. If you find Edgar Lister, you can just make out the remains of the red paint within the inscription, and there are other examples of painted inscriptions elsewhere in the churchyard.

Continuing along the main grass path away from the tower we begin to see changes in memorial style. Many headstones are more elaborate, and we see more imagery and more epitaphs. The monuments are no longer just details of who was buried and their dates. Please feel free to walk among the graves anywhere in the churchyard but do be careful.

To the right is one of four Commonwealth War Graves with its typical simple Portland Stone memorial giving minimal detail. These indicate where a soldier is buried here rather than in France, Belgium or elsewhere. Families could have such a grave or chose to have a son buried in the family grave. We have examples of both. Whether in an official CWG or with the family, both memorials are cared for jointly by CWG commission and The Friends. The first of the CWG headstones is for Gunner J.L. Brook on the right-hand side of the path. Other family headstones tell of those who died in WWI and are buried abroad but remembered here.

As you walk along you may see an open book or bible at the head of a grave. Towards the wall there is a fine example of an Art Deco headstone with an angel praying for the departed.

When you come to the first junction, turn right and just a few headstones down, is one made for George Duncan, the civil engineer, and from a different material. The erosion is so much worse than those of York stone.

Returning to the main path, other graves included kerbstones with or without a raised headstone and pedestal memorials which come in many variations. There is evidence that several of the graves had been surrounded by iron railings, as was the churchyard itself. Soon after this, again on the right, you will see the first of two areas that have been roped off as 'wild area'. This reminds us of what the churchyard was like when the Friends began their work of restoration. The Friends try to reduce substantially such invasive plants as brambles allowing other 'weeds' such as nettles and rosebay willow herb to provide a home to many insects, butterflies and moths. There were many species of bees there and bumblebees have built themselves some nests. Insects like these are important pollinators and are becoming increasingly rare. Nettles can support over 40 kinds of insects which, in turn, overwinter and provide early food for ladybirds, blue tits and other woodland birds. In late summer, they produce lots of seeds for other birds, moths and butterflies. But there has to be a balance! However, weedkillers and other chemicals have not been used in recent times, quite possibly for fifty years.

As you walk along the broad path, do read some of the inscriptions. In some cases, just bare details of the deceased, in others almost a family history. However, there are few indicators of what people did. Soon after the first cross path, to your right and three rows in, is a headstone for Rev Thomas Cox, a Headmaster of Heath Grammar School. To the left is a family grave which includes Arthur Rushworth who died in a tram accident at North Bridge in 1906. In fact, there are two of that name close by. The other died in WWI.

On the left side of the path are two interesting headstones: the first, a large cross, to the Newsome family who lost two sons in WWI, and a little further along an unusual combination of names for the young child, Sharp Shooter. This headstone is leaning at what looks like a precarious angle. It is much more stable than it looks and is checked regularly by Council specialists. You may see examples of where a mother's maiden name is used as a forename, for example Squire in Squire Marsden is his name and not his title!

Just as you turn east along the path you can see, on the left, a memorial to Corporal Joe Willie Shaw who died as a result of a gas attack, and another to Alderman Mark Dawson, a former Mayor of Bradford and his two wives both called Elizabeth. Nearby is a headstone to the Berry family. Janet Berry was a headmistress at the National School. Her name is on the family headstone, which also commemorates two of her nephews who died in WWI.

Beyond here to the north is the new burial ground with burials dating from the 1970s to the present day. Part of this area drains badly and is possibly why there is a bog willow tree here. Be careful if you are tempted to explore to the north of this cross path as some of the land is very uneven. Instead, go past the striking pedestal memorial to Abraham Turner to see Fred Booth's memorial, another casualty of WWI.

Till Carr Cottage was built in 1634 on a site to the west of the church and was moved to its current site around the time that the churchyard was enlarged. The moving, presumably stone by stone, was funded by Evan Charles Sutherland Walker and his wife, the plaque high up on the wall dates this to 1866.

Now, as you turn south and head back to the main entrance, along the main path on your right is a memorial to William Cook, a former headteacher of the National School (now Lightcliffe Primary School) and immediately next to it are the graves of the Hanson family, who were veterinary surgeons.

It is worth going off the path to your left to see the headstone for Dragoon Guard Joseph Naylor, with his sword. He saw service in the Crimean War and is said to have taken his horse, Magpie, there and brought it back – an early *War Horse* story.

Shortly after this one, and alongside the path, are two WWI memorials to Joe Holt and May Hartley, the only woman commemorated amongst the war dead of Lightcliffe. She died as a result of a fall through a trap door whilst working in the Brooke's munitions factory.

On the way round you will have noticed many inscriptions to children who died in infancy. Many more from poor families were buried without a memorial. We believe that they were buried between this path and the boundary wall and the ground then reused in the latter part of last century. Other infants, even when there was no family connection, might be buried in a recently used grave.

Towards the end of this main path, on the left, you will see a "bug hotel" – a luxury 'Des. Res.' with different materials and openings.

You will have seen a number of monuments broken or fallen. Twenty have been restored and, where restoration was not possible, the headstones have been turned over so that the inscriptions can again be read. On your right are two such restored headstones, for Mary Ann Mitchell and Maria Kershaw.

As you come back to the end of the path, on your right-hand side, look for the obelisk memorial partly dedicated to Willie Brooke who died in a railway accident. He was part of the stone and brick company based on St Giles Road. By chance two pieces of brick, used to form the foundation of a nearby headstone, were found with the name 'Brookes' inscribed. Immediately in front is a memorial to Samuel Lord Watkinson. He and his family were major benefactors of local churches (the Lady Chapel in the new church and Northowram Parish church) and of the poor. On the other side of the path is a Calvary-style memorial, dedicated to Ben Skelton Ward. Note the stones representing a hill.

Passing the Till Carr Lane entrance, firstly look at the unusual table-type tomb and then you are back in the 'closed' part of the churchyard and almost all graves are again flat ledger stones with just a few tombs. There is a young yew tree near the entrance.

When you are level with the end of the church, you should find a larger than average grave near to the end of the old church dedicated to the Walker family. They owned most of our area from 1750 to 1870 and many of the big houses. The inscription shows the family moving between Cliff Hill House and Crow Nest Mansion. Next to it is what looks to be the base of a chest tomb. We now believe that some of these grand memorials were removed in the 1970s. An action that would not be allowed today and, probably, was not then.

On the left and almost leaning against the wall is a headstone dedicated to Nancy Midgley. It is unusual in that it is facing west. We do not know if it was erected this way or has been moved.

From here towards the entrance path are many of the old graves. It is interesting to see the styles of carving – many presumably done by local craftsmen by hand – often changing as generations are added to the grave. There are several here dated from the late C17 to the mid-1700s. About 20m from Wakefield Road there is a row of about eight early ledger stones. Look especially for Dorothy with the D backwards!

If you can find the large chest tomb dedicated to Mary Armytage and family then immediately next to it there is a ledger stone for Priscilla Ouldfield 1686. Very faintly you may make out a pair of hands clasped in friendship.

Then look for the Holland tomb which is built on top of ledger stones of earlier family members. Was this a case of showing that the latest family member had done well for himself?

A few rows in from here is the chest tomb of the Guest family. Joshua Guest became famous in 1746 when he successfully commanded Edinburgh Castle against the Jacobite Rebellion (he has a monument in Westminster Abbey).

Just before you leave by the main gate and up against the Wakefield Road wall and near to the noticeboard, do look for Stephen Schofield, the blacksmith whose anvil is now quiet.

We hope that you have enjoyed touring this old and precious place.

'A sanctuary for the living as well as the dead.'

9 Further information and research

If you are interested, our website contains, as we go to print, 55 chapters of family histories including 130 individual articles. From Appleyards and Armytages to Walkers and Woods. We are continuing to add stories as we gain further information.

These stories can be found by following the link 'About the Churchyard' and its drop down menu.

https://www.lightcliffechurchyard.org.uk/about-churchyard/people-of-interest

If you have information about people who were buried in our churchyard, do please contact us.

Your family may have ancestors buried in the churchyard. You can check this out by going to the home page, clicking on Burial Records which takes you to the search page. If you enter the details that you know, the system searches the 11,300 records and gives the details that we have. The details may include dates of death and burial, the location of the grave (as we have indicated from 1867 onwards we know exactly where people are buried, prior to that we only know if there is a gravestone.), a plan of that part of the churchyard and, if there is one, a transcription of the memorial.

If you are unable to visit and want a photograph, please make contact.

A piece of advice when searching, be prepared to try slightly different spellings. A Hinchcliffe today might have been a Hinscliff two hundred years ago. Good luck.

10 Resources and acknowledgements

Records & analysis

The Friends of St Matthew's Churchyard have a burial search facility on their website. Underpinning this is a detailed spreadsheet which contains information on those buried in the churchyard. This is available on request from the Friends.

People buried here

There are around 11,300 buried in the churchyard. We know very little about the majority of them other than their name, date of death and, in many cases, the names of their immediate relatives. It is likely that individual family descendants know more from their own research of family histories.

Others we know considerably more about mainly because they or their families were well known in the locality. In some cases, the Friends have researched in considerable detail the family stories and these are published on the website. This began with a project to mark those who died in WW1 to coincide with its centenary and has since extended to include others buried here or associated with the church. This is being extended on a regular basis.

The Friends also have photographs of all of the memorials.

Resources

- The memorial stones themselves.
- Blackburn Register of Memorial Inscriptions.
- The burial records: legible from 1813, less so previously.
- Carol Cowling's spreadsheet of the post-1867 burials with many grave plots details.
- Ian Philp's plans of the old churchyard, the middle ground, and new burial areas.
- West Yorkshire Archive Service, Wakefield. The records for St Matthew's are WDP47 and for Greetland WDP116/16.

We can, and do, now trace the records and can usually tell whether there is a memorial stone available or not.

Acknowledgements

We are very grateful for the assistance of

Chris Helme, for his original presentation on the 'residents' of the churchyard.
David Glover, for background information on the Walker family and Sutherland Walker.
David Cant, for background information on the Jackson of Coley family.
Steve Crabtree and Diane Halford for the generous use of their research into the Lister and Walker families.
Carol Cowling for her detailed transcriptions of the early burial records.
Andrea Gilpin of Caring for God's Acre; Graham Jackson and Margie Savery, who is related to the Ripley family, for the up-to-date photograph of the memorial in St Mary's and additional information.
Olly Foster and Paul Wood for information on Egton Church.
Memories from some Lightcliffe residents.
The Friends of St Matthew's Churchyard working in partnership with the church's Parochial Church Council.
Rev Kathryn Buck, vicar, and Barbara Smith, churchwarden.

Bob Horne, Chair of Lightcliffe and District Local History Society. This book was his idea and he was the proof reader.

References

Horsfall Turner, J. (1893). *The History of Brighouse, Rastrick and Hipperholme: with Manorial Notes on Coley, Lightcliffe, Northowram, Shelf, Fixby, Clifton and Kirklees.* First published 1893, reprinted Guiseley: MTD Rigg (Publications)1985.
Parker, James. (1904). *Illustrated History from Hipperholme to Tong.* Bradford: Percy Lund, Humphries and Co., Ltd.
St Matthew's Centenary Year. (1975) a short history.
Horsfall Turner, J. (1908) *Lightcliffe Old Chapel; with description of the new church 1529-1908.* Brighouse: John Hartley Ltd.
Morgan, Leslie (1962) *The Story of Lightcliffe Church.*
Saunders, Matthew. *Lightcliffe Old Church, St Matthew's.* former Hon. Director of Friends of Friendless Churches. Reproduced from Volume 45 of the Transactions of the Ancient Monuments Society (TAMS).
Saunders, Matthew, (2010), *Saving Churches.* London: Frances Lincoln Ltd.
Horsfall Turner, J. (1871/2) *Brighouse News* Articles on the history of the church.
Stead, Harold (c.1927) *The Ecclesiastical and other Woodwork of H P Jackson.*
The Yorkshire Post and Leeds Intelligencer, September 22nd 1875
Bretton, R. (1957) *Hipperholme and Lightcliffe.* Halifax Antiquarian Society Transactions.
West Yorkshire Archive, Wakefield. WDP47
The Brighouse News September 25th 1875
Pybus, K.P. *In the Tides of Men.* for more details on the Ripley's in Bradford & Bedstone.
Leleux, L.A. (1971) *Brookes' Industrial Railways.* Oakwood Press.

Yorke, Trevor, (2010) *Gravestones, Tombs & Memorials*. Newbury: Countryside Books.

Liddington, Jill, (2019) *Female Fortune, Land, Gender and Authority*. Rivers Oram Press.

Photographs of old church before demolition courtesy of Historic England

Friends of Friendless Churches for colour photos of demolition in progress and the church from the north.

Malcolm Bull's Calderdale Companion.

The 'In search of Ann Walker' website.

Court opinion sought. John Walker & his widow Fanny. WYA CN100/2.

Original parish records on Ancestry and FindmyPast.

Prerogative & Exchequer Courts of York Probate Index, 1688-1858 on FindmyPast.

FOSMC website. The Friends of St Matthew's Churchyard website, www.lightcliffechurchyard.org, contains a lot of additional material both on the churchyard and the lives of those associated with it. Visit About the Churchyard and look for People of Interest, and old church and archive material.

11 Appendices

Plaques, tablets and pew plates

Plaques

There are six of these. They were fixed to pews along the main aisle commemorating some of those buried under the church. They are stored in the vestry of St Matthew's Church. All are made of brass and now covered with a heavy patina. Four quite plain ones were dedicated to John and Elizabeth Holmes (1741 & 1775), Samuel and Rebekah Walker of Sleadsike (1746 & 1745), Judith Wainhouse (1778) and John Gill Sleadsike (1787).

Two are slightly more elaborate and were mounted on the walls of the church. These commemorate Mary Walker, eldest daughter of William Walker, of Crow Nest, who died September 13th 1822, aged 76 years and his youngest daughter Ann Walker who died October 29th 1847, aged 90 years.

Tablets

There are four memorials kept within the Tower.

Rev Richard Sutcliffe and his wife, Martha. The inscription is in Latin with many ecclesiastical abbreviations. It does, however, paint a picture of a dedicated parish priest.

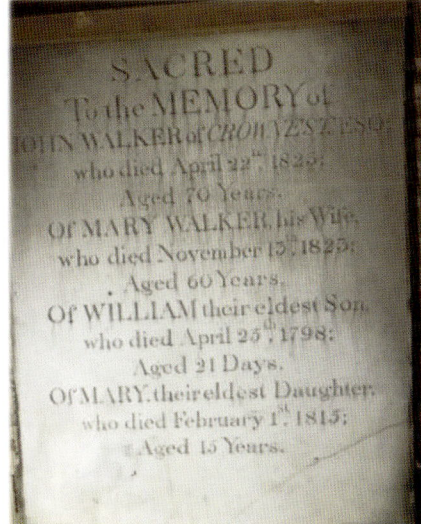

The second is

Sacred to the memory of John Walker of Crow Nest, Esq, died April 22nd 1823 aged 70 years.

Of Mary Walker, his wife, who died November 13th 1823 aged 60 years.

Of William their eldest son, who died April 25th 1798, aged 21 days

Of Mary, their eldest daughter, who died on February 1st 1815 aged 15years

The third is that for Ann Walker and the image appears earlier.

> *In memory of Ann Walker, of Cliffe Hill, who was born May 20th 1803, died February 25th 1854, and is buried beneath the pulpit in this church; and her niece Mary who died in 1846, aged 15, and is buried in this churchyard; and of her nephew George Sackville, who died in 1843 aged 12, and John Walker, who died in 1836 aged one year, and who are buried at Kirk Michael, Ross-shire, children of George Mackay and Elizabeth Sutherland. ECASW 1862*

Finally, though split into two parts, is that of John Walker.

Several other tablets are mentioned in J. Horsfall Turner's history of the church. It is assumed that they were vandalised before the church was demolished.

Joseph Swaine left money for the poor of this parish:

> *In memory of Rev Joseph Swaine, B.D., a native of this chapelry, late incumbent of Beeston, in the parish of Leeds. He departed this life on the 18th November 1831, aged 77 years.*

The one for George Mackay Sutherland read:

> *In memory of George Mackay Sutherland of Aberarder, Inverness-shire, Captain of His Majesty's 13th Regiment of Light Dragoons who was born November 10th 1798, died April 22nd 1847 and is buried in the churchyard; and of Elizabeth, his wife, daughter of John Walker, of Crow Nest, who was born November 10th 1801, died December 28th 1844 and is buried in Wimbledon, Surrey.*

There was also one for Rev Robert Wilkinson.

The Alfred Ripley tablet was moved in 1884 and is now displayed at St Mary's Church, Bedstone, Shropshire.

Pew plaques

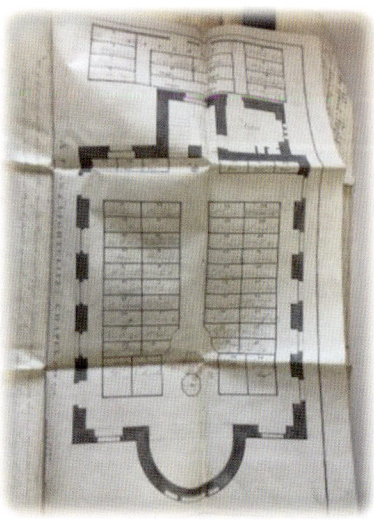

At the time the church was being rebuilt a faculty was applied for the arrangements of the pews. The pews were sold to people of wealth and a brass plaque was attached. The plaques, in 1779, cost 1s 6d for one name, 2s for two and in proportion for more. The engraver was John Butterworth of Leeds.

As an example, William Rookes paid £8 7s 9d for pew number 45 in 1779 which included the 2s for the engraved plate. The receipt was issued by William Walker as churchwarden after it had been processed through the Archbishop's Ecclesiastical Court. Rookes allocated it to his farm, in Norwood Green. By 1867 it had been transferred to directors of the Low Moor Company.

Thomas Thornhill bought a pew, also in 1779, for £10 15s, which was allotted to his farm, also in Norwood Green. Again, it was William Walker who organised this. The letter agreeing to this was sent from Berkley Square, London, on February 23rd and sealed with his coat of arms. He lived locally at Fixby Hall which is still part of the Thornhill estate. The pew is not identifiable.

Some of the plaques are the originals, some were added when there was a change of ownership.

The plan shows a central pulpit rather than the dual arrangement of 1863 onwards. There is a gallery with further numbered pews. There is no sign in the Archive of the plan of the galleries on either side of the church. The pews, certainly from 1863, were boxed. Quite possibly they always were.

Most of the plates survive and are in the West Yorkshire Archive, Wakefield.

Often when a house or farm was sold the pew was part of the sale. When the Crow Nest Estate went for auction in 1867, 26 lots (out of 280) included a pew at St Matthew's. Several more included pews at St John's Coley. The former are detailed at the end of this article. When Joseph Armytage was selling Green House to Ann Walker (and renting it back) it included Pew 31.

Anne Lister rented the gallery pew allocated to Mytholm (The Stag) for a guinea per year. From the descriptions in her diaries in September 1834 it was in the front row on the north side nearest to the west gallery. This is the pew that she had upholstered in green.

The table below relates to the plan from the 1779 faculty.

Gallery			
4 Tho. Thornhill Esq			**8** William Walker Esq
3	**5** The curate of Lightcliffe	**12**	**9** James Gledhill Esq
2	**6** Singers	**13** Singers	**10** Mr Macauley
1 possibly Banks Farm	**7** Singers	**14** Singers	**11** Organist

Main body of the church			
23-25 Poor		**26-28** Poor	
13 *illegible*	**12** Curate	**29** Lister? Whitehall	**50** William Walker
15 *Illegible*	**10** Wm Stocks Till Carr	**31** Joseph Armytage Green House Crow Nest	**48** J Foster Cliff Hill

16 Lister, Sutcliffe Wood Organist	**9** J&T Aspinall Hove Edge Mann's Farm	**32** Radcliffe Townend Farm	**47** J Smithson Lidgate
17 Mr Smith ?	**8** Curate & William Walker Upper Cliff Hill	**33** Sam Armytage	**46** Fourness ? Lower Rooks
18 Curate *illegible*	**7** William Walker Crow Nest then Thomas MacCauley Laverack Hall	**34** Matilda Tate Yew Trees 1861	**45** Dawson, Hardy Low Moor Works
19 Richard Riddlesden Upper Rooks	**6** William Walker Knowl Top	**35** Sunderland Lower Green	**44** Nicholls & Macauley
20 William Priestley German House Farm & Rev Rob Wilkinson, White Hall Farm	**5** Samuel Armytage then J Foster, Cliff Hill 1867	**36** Smith & Hoyle House	**43** William Radcliffe Upper Crow Nest
21 Lister? Lower Crow Nest?	**4** Curate Mrs Holmes Smith House	**37** Nicholls & Macauley	**42** Walker Norwood Green
22 Langtry? Priestley	**3** Curate & Master of Hipperholme Free School	**38** Curate (half) *Illegible* (half)	**41** *illegible*
1 William Walker	**2** Curate Nicholls & Macauley Slead Hall	**39** Mrs Holmes Smith House	**40** William Walker Crow Nest
Altar			

In addition, the following brasses have no pew number.

James Walker Ledgate	John Holland Slead House	Longbottom Lower German House. (1871 census Thomas)	J Foster, Cliffe Hill 1867 *This is 19 Gallery.* *Tied to Cliffe Hill in* *1867 Auction.*

These are examples of the better-preserved ones.

More details of the ownership of the pews are to be found on FOSMC website.

Charities associated with the church.

The Benefactors Board which used to hang in the old church is now stored within the tower, vertically, and attached to battens. It measures about 12' x 3' 9" and looks to be oak with gold leaf script. It has a ladder fixed diagonally across it making parts difficult to read.

Benefactions to the Poor of Hipperholme & Hipperholme *

Benefactors	When left	Will or Deed	How to be applied	Whence issuing	Amount produce	Benefactors	When left	Will or Deed	How to be applied	Whence issuing	Amount produce
Mr Tho. Whitely of Cinder Hills	Nov 17th AD 1631	Left by Will	To the Governors & Trustees of Hipperholme Free Grammer School, in trust, the sum of forty shillings per annum to be distributed to the poor of Hipperholme on St Thomas's Day in every year.	Charged on Yew Trees Farm, the property of Josh Lister Esq, Harley Head Farm, the property of William Walker Esq. A farm in the village of Hipperholme the property of Mr Chas Dearden.	£. s. d. 10. 0 10. 0 1. 0. 0	Michl. Gibson Esq of Slead Hall	AD 1738	Left by Will	To be distributed by the Ministers & Churchwardens on every Sunday in the year for ever at Lightcliffe Chapel the value of 1 shilling in bread to 12 persons residing at Hough Edge & Upper Lane. This is charged upon the Pear Tree Farm at Lightcliffe.		£. s. d. 2. 12. 0
Nath. Waterhouse of Halifax	AD 1642	Left by Will & which has since been confirmed by Act of Parliament in the year 1777	To 16 inhabitants of the Town & Parish of Halifax under the title of Governors & Trustees certain estates lying in the Town & Parish of Halifax in trust for various purposes &, amongst others, one is for apportioning a part of the revenue of the said estates amongst the Churchwardens & Overseers of the town & 9 other Hamlets	The annual amount varies, the Portion paid in March 1809 to the Overseer of Hipperholme was.	22. 0. 0.	The Rev'd Richard Sutcliffe AM late Curate of Lightcliffe	AD 1782	Left by Will	To Mr William Walker at Crow Nest, the Ministers & Churchwardens of Lightcliffe & their successors in trust 20 shillings per annum to be by them distributed at Lightcliffe Chapel on Christmas Day to 20 poor persons residing in Hipperholme cum Brighouse having no Parish relief.	This is charged upon an estate at Sheard Green.	1. 0. 0
Sam'. Sunderland of Harden Beck near Bingley	AD 1671	Gave by Deed	To the Governors & Trustees of Hipperholme Free Grammer School, a farm called Birks Close near Norwood Green, the annual produce of which is to be distributed at the School to the most indigent of & within the Township of Hipperholme-cum-Brighouse on Midsummer's Day & St Thomas's Day in every year by the Ministers, Churchwardens & Overseers of the Poor of Lightcliffe & Coley.	This farm was let upon a lease of 200 years at £8 per annum which is expired. The Trustees have borrowed money for rebuilding the House & Barn so that the distribution continues until the Debt is paid off.	8. 0. 0.	Mr Jas. Gledhill of Smith House in Lightcliffe	AD 1789	Left by Will	To Mr William Walker of Crow Nest & his successors in trust the sum of 40 shillings, one half to be laid out in linen cloth for 8 poor women & the other half to be applied to the benefit of Sunday Schools but if the Sunday Schools be discontinued then the 20 shillings to be distributed to the poor on Christmas Day in every year.		

| | | | | | | William Walker | AD 1810 | Left by Will | Extract from Will: I give my Executors & Trustees & their heirs one annuity clear yearly rent or sum of £10 upon trust that they or the survivors or survivors of them or his heirs shall do distribute the same at the Chapel of Lightcliffe on Christmas Day every year for ever; to & amongst such poor persons of the Township of Hipperholme aforesaid as they shall think fit the sum of two pounds part thereof being the interest of £50 paid to me under the will of the late James Gledhill & the residue thereof I declare to be donated from myself. | This bequest was under the Statute of Mortmain. | |

There are a few letters or numbers after the second Hipperholme* but they are difficult to make out.

Hipperholme Free Grammer School: "Grammer" is the spelling used in each case.

The Statute of Mortmain was an ancient legal restraint dating from the reign of Edward I.

Mr Thomas Whitely of Cinder Hills near Coley, 1631. His charity was amalgamated with the Sunderland Charity in 1885 and finally closed in 2004. Like Nathaniel Waterhouse, he refused a knighthood in 1626 from Charles I, who was raising money independently of Parliament, and paid the penalty ('composition') of £10. In 1895 the income amounted to £2. Harley Head Farm and Yew Tree Farm contributing 10s each and Dearden's Farm a pound.

Samuel Sunderland of Harden Beck near Bingley. 1641 (1599-1676). He also owned Coley Hall and built The Sisters' House at Priestley Green. He was a major benefactor in our area and provided land for Hipperholme Grammar School, a farm as the schoolhouse and a legacy for the Sunderland Scholarships. The charity was for the poor of the chapelries of Coley and Lightcliffe. The income came from both the farm and the sale of the coal from under part of the farmland. It appears to have generated £57 per year around 1904.

By 1895 these two charities were being administered as one by the overseers of the poor, who kept a list of recipients. Vacancies were filled at the discretion of the trustees. All recipients, unless infirm, had to attend in person to receive between 2s and 5s.

Nathaniel Waterhouse of Halifax, 1642 (1586-1645). He was a major benefactor to the area, leaving money to the poor, the clergy and even for the upkeep of roads, including Watergate in Hipperholme. His composition was £13 6s 8d when he declined a knighthood.

Michael Gibson Esq. of Slead Hall, 1738 (1666-1738) He lived in Slead House, Brighouse and bought Giles House, Hove Edge in 1702, both of which he altered. His first marriage, 1696, to Elizabeth Lord was in St Matthew's (Eastfield Chapel). Initially the bequest was to benefit 12 poor residents in Hove Edge and Upper Lane. It took the form of a distribution of bread and was administered by the minister and churchwardens. It was based on income from Pear Tree Farm, opposite to the new St Matthew's Church. By 1904 the owner of the farm is Rev J.W. Hall, and the management has been transferred to the overseers of the poor. At this time there were no applicants from Hove Edge and Upper Green. Three recipients lived in Norwood Green and on Bramley Lane. It was known as Lightcliffe Bread Charity.

Rev Rich Sutcliffe, 1782, is mentioned earlier in the book. The property generating the income for this bequest, Sheard Green, was a small farm in Hove Edge on Well Green Lane, diagonally opposite to Nether House. The farm was purchased for the Curate in 1749 from the Queen Anne Bounty. When the property transferred to Richard Kershaw, the bequest was still being paid.

Mr James Gledhill of Smith House in Lightcliffe, 1789 (1713-1792).

The William Walkers are mentioned earlier in this book. The board dates this bequest as 1810. This would be William, (1749-1809), the son of the William who was heavily involved in the rebuilding of the church. As other benefactors have references to a William Walker and are dated around 1780, these suggest that it is William the father. In all probability, the younge William's bequest was a continuation or restatement of an existing bequest. Ann Walker took over the responsibility for her grandfather's and uncle's bequest. There is a record book in the Archive showing the distribution of money from Ann Walker's legacy to the poor over several years.

The total income is indicated as being worth £47. Inflation was low during this period judging by the similarity of sums over a period of 200 years. At a vestry meeting in 1826 each of the charities was discussed. Most were satisfactorily being received and distributed. However, a concern was raised regarding part of the Thomas Whiteley charity. Whilst the Yew Trees and Harley Head incomes were accounted for, that from Dearden's Farm (then in the possession of Susan Holroyd) had not been received for 13 years. It was resolved to report this to the Commissioners for Charities. It was subsequently paid. There was also a shortfall from the Birk's Close Farm in the occupation of Joseph Brook but there is no indication of whether this was resolved.

James Holland of Slead House had established a charitable giving of 6s 8d on a farm in Norwood Green to be paid to the poor and needy of that village.

Squire's Legacy. Sydney Squire died in 1900 having been the landlord of The Hare and Hounds, Hipperholme, for 30 years. In his will he provided for his widow until her death (1903) and the £300 from his estate was to be invested by the vicar and churchwardens of Lightcliffe to be given to the poor of Hipperholme over the age of 60. The initial investment was in Bradford Corporation Stock. This was to be in the form of flour and coal to be distributed at Christmas. Both Sydney and his wife, Eliza, are buried in the churchyard.

Over the course of time, the value of these bequests decreased because of inflation and the introduction of the welfare state. All of these charities had been wound up towards the end of the last century or early in this.

Index to people mentioned in the book. A name in italics means that they were buried or remembered in the churchyard or either of the two churches. More details can be found for most of these individuals on the Burial Search facility on the website where a transcription of their name on a memorial inscription may be found if one is available.

The Ann Walker memorial plaque

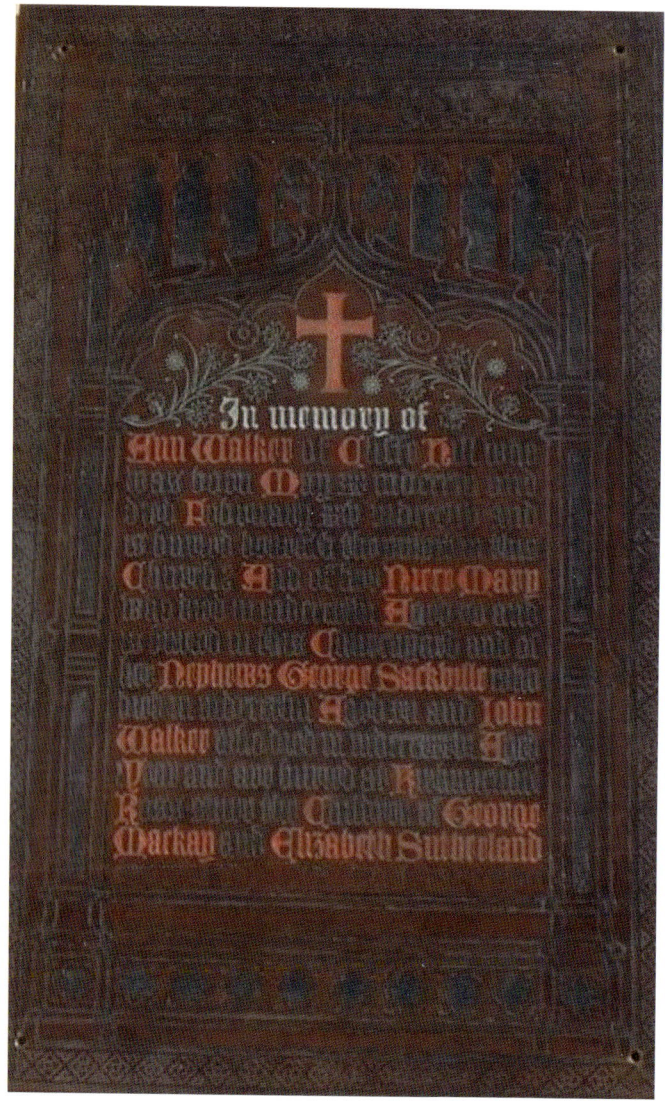

recently restored in the Grantham workshops of
Skillingtons, Historic Building Repair and Restoration.

Very kindly paid for by a crowd funded initiative led by **In Search of Ann Walker**,
a collaborative group of people, interested in bringing to light details of Ann Walker's life.

Courtesy of **Friends of Friendless Churches**.